Human Nature

Human Nature

A Guide to Managing Workplace Relations

GREG CLYDESDALE
Lincoln University, New Zealand

Routledge
Taylor & Francis Group

LONDON AND NEW YORK

First published 2013 by Gower Publishing

2 Park Square, Milton Park, Abingdon, Oxon OX14 4RN
711 Third Avenue, New York, NY 10017, USA

Routledge is an imprint of the Taylor & Francis Group, an informa business

First issued in paperback 2016

Gower Applied Business Research
Our programme provides leaders, practitioners, scholars and researchers with thought provoking, cutting edge books that combine conceptual insights, interdisciplinary rigour and practical relevance in key areas of business and management.

British Library Cataloguing in Publication Data
A catalogue record for this book is available from the British Library.

The Library of Congress has cataloged the printed edition as follows:
Clydesdale, Greg.
  Human nature : a guide to managing workplace relations / by Greg Clydesdale.
    pages cm
  Includes bibliographical references and index.
  ISBN 978-1-4724-1679-7 (hardback)
  1. Industrial relations. 2. Organizational behavior. 3. Interpersonal relations. I. Title.

  HD6971.C57 2013
  658.3'145–dc23

                                                                2013023966

ISBN 978-1-4724-1679-7 (hbk)
ISBN 978-1-138-24756-7 (pbk)

Contents

Lists of Figures and Tables

Figures

Tables

Preface

My first management job was a shock! Nothing I had learned at business school prepared me for it. The subjects I studied at university were far away from the day-to-day people management that characterized my work. It was almost as if universities and companies were on two different planets.

Years later, I found myself teaching management at a university, and I swore I would never leave my students so ill equipped. In preparing my classes, I initially put aside the textbook and began asking colleagues in business what they expected from their future managers. Their answers varied, but they had the same underlying theme – they wanted to employ managers with an ability to deal with people.

Not surprisingly, recent research shows that those with well-developed social skills earn higher salaries. It is not just in companies' interest for managers to have better social skills; it also helps individuals advance their careers.

Universities have long been criticized for their failure to provide social skills, and a lot of progress has been made since I first graduated, particularly in the area of communication and emotional intelligence. However, gaps remain.

One of the biggest gaps is in the area of 'human nature'. Many businesspeople told me that the key to success was understanding human nature, but this is a concept that business schools ignore. The complexity of the topic means it sits in the 'too hard basket', and our future managers are deprived of the most important part of their education.

For me, this problem presented an irresistible challenge, and before long, I was questioning business colleagues about the sort of problems they were confronting on a daily basis. Common patterns appeared, and common human traits were at play. This allowed me to identify the most common traits that regularly impacted on the work of managers.

Most of the traits are well known to business scholars, and this book rests on a strong body of academic research. However, some of the traits are not commonly taught in business schools, such as 'the limited span of absolute judgement'. This concept is similar to 'bounded rationality', in that it recognizes the limitations of the human mind. However, limited span of absolute judgement is more precise, and asks managers to seriously consider the mental limits of their colleagues and themselves. Having a clearer concept of our limits can allow us to develop strategies to mitigate our own weaknesses, and understand the shortfalls of those we deal with.

With an understanding of human nature, we can develop relationship management strategies. However, there is one other important ingredient. As I delved deeper in to the topic, I came to realize that the patterns I observed in others also existed in me. To manage others effectively, I had to accept my own cognitive, emotional and motivational limitations. This requires 'self-knowing', and this is the hardest part of the process because of all the cognitive biases that distort our self-perception.

After years of collecting information, I felt I had a model that I could test on my students. The students in my Professional Studies class are a mature group who already hold management positions. It was my job to teach them 'leadership', a subject characterized by a number of different theories. At the beginning of the course, I gave my students the model of human nature. They were then told to keep a diary in which they analysed their workplace interactions in light of the human characteristics taught in class. At the end of the course, I asked these students to evaluate how useful the model (and diary) had been. It was a great success, with students claiming it greatly assisted their work. As one manager stated: 'I am thinking about it constantly, long after I posted the final assignment.'

Not only did the model offer a practical and useful way to improve management performance, it actually complemented the leadership theory they were taught later in the year. It provided a basic view of human nature on which the later theories could build.

This book argues that understanding human nature is the key to good management. Such is this understanding's importance in enhancing business and personal success, I believe it should be the basis of all business education.

Acknowledgements

I would like to thank Julian Pillidge, Annie Angus, Barbara Plester, Mohini Sukhapure, Andy Moyle and the large number of people who allowed me to use their experiences to illustrate management issues. For the sake of confidentiality, I cannot mention their names, but they know who they are.

1

Human Nature and Management

Education is a progressive discovery of our own ignorance.
Will Durant[1]

A manager of a hospital department once told me how he thought he was doing one of his staff a favour. Frank, the staff member in question, had been pressuring the manager to commit resources to a project:

> *Frank convinced me that the project was a good idea, and I hired a consultant to do it, but when I told this to Frank, I got a very subdued response. I know he wanted a lead role in the project, but I simply couldn't release him from his duties.*

Frank later confessed: 'It felt like an attack on my ability. To make things worse, the consultant he hired was someone I had earlier told about the project. It was a real slap in the face.' After this, Frank's commitment dropped. It seems strange that a simple thing like allocating work can affect someone's self-esteem and sense of belonging to an organization, particularly given that his boss was actually doing what Frank wanted, but people are complex. Consider the next situation, told to me by the owner of a property managing company:

> *We have Raewyn attending to letting apartments in one building and John handling letting in the other. Each are on different forms of remuneration. Each has made remarks about the other's income, and the matter was raised again today. Whilst each accepted their roles as offered to them, they are now drawn towards comparisons in establishing their own sense of fairness or equity in their work situations, yet their basic positions are more diverse than they are similar, and their ultimate worths as to how they can develop as strategic assets for our company are very different.*

---

1   Durant, W. and Durant, A. (1965). 'Books: The Great Gadfly', *Time Magazine*, 8 October (review of *The Age of Voltaire*).

I have endeavoured to gently display this to them, but it is interesting
how people can be happy and motivated in their role one day, and yet
with no change to the terms and conditions of their work environment,
become unhappy and de-motivated the next day simply through
inferring that a colleague is more advantaged.

Humans are weird! They can be emotional, irrational and often unpredictable, yet as their manager, it is your job to get the best out of them. In fact, they are often the key to your success. Sadly, humans do not come with an instruction manual which lists their technical specifications.

Given that people are the most important resource in your business, it is a huge omission to have no conception of human nature. Your management success is strongly dependent on the relationships you build with your workers, colleagues, bosses and suppliers. However, there is no model of human nature to guide you, perhaps because human nature is so complex.

This book is based on the premise that the key to good management is understanding human nature and interpersonal relations. But what is human nature? It will be useful at this stage to provide a definition. If we are looking at one person, we refer to their nature as their 'personality'. Psychologists define personality as 'consistent patterns of behaviour over time for an individual'. If we are to look at all people, we could define human nature as the aggregated personality of all humans. In which case, we could define human nature as 'consistent patterns of behaviour for the human species'.

The concept of 'human nature' suggests that people throughout the world are born with certain characteristics in common, but is that a fair assumption, given the way cultures can mould behaviour? Clearly, we cannot ignore the role of culture, which shapes specific motives and behaviour. For that reason, many of the world's great thinkers have stated that there is no such thing as human nature. This raises an important question: if the world's greatest thinkers are not sure if there is such a thing as human nature, how can managers rely on this concept?

Is There Such a Thing as Human Nature?

Perhaps the most famous management text to address the concept of human nature was Douglas McGregor's *The Human Side of Enterprise*.[2] In this book,

---

2   McGregor, D. (1960). *The Human Side of Enterprise*, New York: McGraw-Hill.

McGregor detailed two theories (X and Y) which made detailed assumptions about the characteristics of workers. Theory X assumed that workers dislike work, avoid responsibility and lack motivation. Managers who hold this view of human nature rely heavily on threats and coercion to achieve organizational goals. Their workplaces are characterized by mistrust, restrictive supervision and a punitive atmosphere.

In contrast, Theory Y has a more positive view of human nature. It assumes that workers welcome responsibility, can enjoy work and can be highly motivated. Managers who hold a Theory Y view of human nature are more likely to develop a climate of trust and create an environment that enables employees to develop their abilities. McGregor favoured Theory Y. He said: 'It is important that management abandon limiting assumptions like those of Theory X.'

The two conflicting views of human nature that McGregor describes reflect a debate among philosophers as to the true nature of humans, in particular whether we are good or bad, and how we should be led. From the ancient Greeks to Karl Marx, philosophers have been tasked with linking human nature to productive activity. In the rest of this section, we will consider their views.

Among the Greek philosophers, the Sophists' view can be loosely connected with McGregor's Theory X, in that they both share a negative view of human nature. In ancient Greece, the Sophists earned their living teaching the children of wealthy Greek families. In fact, the word 'sophist' means teacher. The Sophists believed that humans were selfish egotists. People may live with others in societies, but they are not naturally predisposed to this. Humans are selfish, and living together in human societies is necessary only to provide security and maintain order.

Socrates opposed this, pounding the streets of Athens propounding a more positive view of human nature. He believed humans are naturally social people who are willing to consider others. In fact, he believed that we gain happiness by living a moral and ethical life. Socrates believed that we must recognize our true nature and learn the art of how to live an ethical life. If we ignore this, and selfishly pursue power and pleasure, we will not find happiness.

For Socrates, a good life was a moral life – something he did not see in the rulers of Athens at the time, whom he attacked for their selfish pursuit of power and pleasure. However, these attacks put him out of favour, and he was eventually tried for crimes of 'religious impiety' and 'corrupting young people'. Found guilty, he was put to death – an action that suggested people may have negative characteristics in their nature.

Socrates' student Plato shared his teacher's positive view, but developed a more sophisticated view of humans which suggested we have elements of both Theory X and Theory Y. Plato believed that human nature had two conflicting components. The first was an appetitive beast driven by basic bodily desires such as food, drink, sex, and emotions such as anger and ambition. These drives were similar to those found in animals, but fortunately, according to Plato, humans had another component that raised them above the animals. Humans have an intellectual soul or psyche that enables us to act rationally. This rational soul gives people the ability to think and control their basic passions. However, it is not always easy to control our basic desires. Humans can find it hard to act virtuously, especially when it comes to controlling sexual desires. However, on the whole, Plato believed that our rational abilities enabled us to live a good life, but to attain our potential, humans needed to be educated. With this in mind, Plato established the first 'academy'.

Aristotle studied at Plato's Academy, accepted his teacher's view of human nature, and like Socrates, believed that humans want to live a virtuous life. A coward will not find happiness, but a courageous man will. Aristotle further developed these theories in his book *Nichomachean Ethics*, in which he advocated the concept 'eudemonia' – the idea that we should strive towards excellence. He argued that we must be true to our inner self and strive to be the best that we can be.

This has implications for management. It implies that if you help your staff to achieve their potential, they are more likely to display virtuous behaviours. Of course, Aristotle did not speak in terms of management, but the leadership role is important, and he addresses this when he speaks of government. The government should create an environment in which people can fulfil their nature. This requires laws and customs that complement our social instincts. If these are provided, humans will act virtuously.

Aristotle believed there were differences among humans. Women and slaves were inferior, lacked the intellectual ability to make free rational choices and were driven by their basic animal urges. Not that they were completely lacking in intelligence. If they could not think, 'slaves would not be able to execute their master's orders, but their rational capabilities are not at a level that enables self rule'.[3]

The debate over whether humans were good or bad continued into the Middle Ages, when two great Christian philosophers held different opinions. The first was St Augustine (AD 354–430). Augustine was influenced by the biblical story of Adam and Eve. He believed that God had created people to live in peace, but human nature was altered by the sins of Adam and Eve. Their 'original sin' had consequences for all humans born thereafter. Humans are born evil with an inclination to sin, and are driven by evil to break God's law.

The Christian view changed in the thirteenth century, when Europeans rediscovered the works of Aristotle. An Italian priest now known as St Thomas Aquinas (1225–1274) incorporated Aristotle's thoughts into the Christian belief system. St Thomas accepted the classical belief that men have an ability to reason, and this allows them to control their basic urges. It is this ability to reason that raises humans above the animals, but St Thomas gave reason a spiritual dimension. Not only does reason raise man above the biological realm, as Aristotle had asserted, reason unites man with God.

The new Christian view of human nature was very different from that espoused by St Augustine. While Augustine saw sin and evil as the defining characteristics of mankind, St Thomas believed reason was the defining feature, and that reason drove men towards virtue. St Thomas did not deny men's sinfulness, but we have an ability to choose, and because of our sense of reason, human nature is essentially good.

To some philosophers, the selfish nature of man was obvious to anyone who opened their eyes. The Englishman Thomas Hobbes (1588–1679) thought our daily actions showed ample evidence of our distrust of others: 'What opinion he has of his fellow subjects, when he rides armed: of his fellow citizens when he locks his doors: and of his children and servants when he locks his chests?'[4]

Thomas Hobbes lived through the English Civil War, an experience which exposed him to the worst of human nature. It was obvious that humans were driven by self-preservation. He personally witnessed how people could

---

3   Frank, J. (2004). 'Citizens, Slaves and Foreigners: Aristotle on Human Nature'. *American Political Science Review*, 98(1), 91–104.
4   Hobbes, T. (1966). 'Leviathan, or the Matter form and Power of a Commonwealth, ecclesiastical and Civil', in W. Molesworth (ed.). *The English Works of Thomas Hobbes of Malmesbury*, London: John Bohn, p. 114.

take advantage of others for their own gain. In his eyes, humans were self-interested, anti-social, power-seeking animals. They are no different from any other animal that is driven by basic biological urges. Hobbes did not believe that our ability to reason enabled us to control these urges. Our intellectual abilities merely made it possible to satisfy our basic urges.

Of course Hobbes also witnessed times when humans showed compassion and generosity, but he believed that even these were self-motivated. He believed that when we show compassion to people in need, we are conscious that one day we may be in the same situation, so we act with generosity in the hope that people will do the same for us. Our generosity creates a standard of behaviour that will protect ourselves if we are in the same situation. We are generous, but our motive is pure self-interest.

Another influential thinker who thought humans were selfish was Adam Smith, Professor of Moral Philosophy at the University of Glasgow. Smith agreed that humans were selfish, but unlike Hobbes, thought that this was not necessarily a bad thing. When people are motivated by self-interest, they work hard and show initiative. As people selfishly pursue wealth, they will produce the goods and services that other people need, and in that way, help the economy grow. This should be good for everyone. If the government wants community well-being to improve, it should allow these selfish forces free rein in the economy.

In Smith's eyes, it was not a sin to be selfish, it was merely a feature of human nature that, if channelled correctly, could benefit society. Smith published these thoughts in his book *The Wealth of Nations*, published in 1776, the same year that the American Declaration of Independence was signed. Consequently, his book was to have a great influence on political thinking in the United States.

Another philosopher who had a great impact on the United States was the Englishman John Locke (1632–1704), who advanced a view that profoundly altered the way we conceive of human nature. He proposed that there was no such thing as human nature; we are born with no pre-existing knowledge, and it is life experience that determines what we know. He described the human mind as a blank sheet of paper upon which experience writes.[5] This view came to be known as the 'blank slate' (*tabula rasa*) theory of mind, and it opened up

5   Nelson B.R. (1982). *Western Political Thought: from Socrates to the Age of Ideology*. Englewood Cliffs, NJ: Prentice-Hall, p. 162.

a huge debate over whether human personality and behaviour are shaped by nature or nurture. For Locke, the answer was nurture.

Locke did not believe that humans were inherently bad. He believed that God gave humans the ability to reason, and as we learn, we soon determine the correct way to live our life. We discover the moral laws that apply to all people – what Locke called 'natural law'. He believed that in the natural world, people were equal and independent, with a natural right to 'Life, health, Liberty, or Possessions'. This way of thinking influenced the writers of the US Declaration of Independence, who wrote how every man has the right to 'life, liberty and the pursuit of happiness'.

It may be a surprise to discover that the father of communism shared some of John Locke's views on human nature. Like Locke, Karl Marx (1818–1883) favoured the nurture argument, and discarded the idea that we are born with a pre-determined nature. He accepted that humans are born with some core biological foundations such as eating, drinking and procreating, but beyond that, human nature is shaped by the society we live in. Marx believed that each society produces its own needs, and these shape the way that human's develop. Someone raised in a tribal society will have a different nature from someone in a capitalist society. They will think and behave differently, and develop different social relationships.[6]

Marx did notice one distinguishing feature that made us different from other species. Humans are intrinsically creative, with an ability to produce and change their physical environment. It is true that many animals also produce and shape their environment, such as bees, beavers and ants, but they only produce to meet their personal needs and those of their families. In contrast, humans act productively even when their physical needs are satisfied. Humans are wonderfully creative, and may work simply to create beauty.[7]

According to Marx, humans welcome work. In fact, it can become the centre of our lives, shaping our identity and helping us to achieve self-realization. Work can be a natural act of self-expression and creativity. The problem was, under the capitalist system, these benefits had been subsumed to the pursuit of money. People ended up working for the capitalist classes that owned the factories, and their labour became a de-humanizing commodity.

---

6   Ibid., p. 315.
7   Marx, K. and Engels, F. (1970). *German Ideology*, ed. C.J. Arthur, London: Lawrence and Wishart.

Instead of being enjoyable, work was dreary, and humans were not able to express their true selves. Consequently, Marx favoured a revolution in the relations of production. The capitalist society should be overthrown, and replaced with a communist system which gave people greater freedom in how they produced.[8] Under this system, a worker could 'do one thing today and another tomorrow, to hunt in the morning, to fish in the afternoon, rear cattle in the evening'.[9]

There would be no decline in productivity because our natural instincts to create would drive the economy, creating a society of abundance. The socialist nations that appeared during the twentieth century followed Karl Marx, who stated that human behaviour was shaped by the society in which people lived.[10] They rejected any idea that human nature was inherited.

Western nations also rejected 'biological' theories that suggested human nature was inherited. The *tabula rasa* view put forward by John Locke was reinforced by a number of studies, such as one by Margaret Mead which showed free-living adolescents living a stress-free life in Samoa. These studies suggested that society could have a huge impact in the way humans develop. The influential behavioural psychologist John Watson also helped to promulgate such beliefs, arguing that 'there is no such thing as inheritance of capacity, talent, temperament, mental constitution and characteristics'.[11] In the second half of the twentieth century, the debate between nature and nurture definitely favoured 'nurture'. If 'human nature' was not found in management textbooks, it was because academics did not believe in human nature.

The social sciences became dominated by a view that anthropologist John Tooby and psychologist Leda Cosmides called the Standard Social Sciences Model (SSSM).[12] This saw humans as a 'general learning machine for picking up what is in the environment'. It took the view that the human mind was a blank slate containing 'nothing but some motor functions, a few drives and a general learning mechanism'. It was society that determined human action, and all behaviour was a result of social conditioning. This would suggest that

---

8   Trigg, R. (1988). *Ideas of Human Nature: An Historical Introduction*, Oxford: Blackwell.
9   Marx and Engels (1970), 53.
10   Gintis, H. (2007). 'David J. Buller. 2005. Adapting Minds: Evolutionary Psychology and the Persistent Quest for Human Nature' (book review). *Journal of Bioeconomics*, 9(2), 191–200.
11   Watson, J.B. (1925). *Behaviorism*, New York: W.W. Norton.
12   Tooby, J. and Cosmides, L. (1992). The Psychological Foundations of Culture', in J.H. Barkow, L. Cosmides and J. Tooby (eds), *The Adapted Mind*, Oxford: Oxford University Press, pp. 19–136.

managers and leaders could have great influence over their workers' actions, and that there were no inherent traits they needed to consider.

This view was inherently logical given the large number of studies showing that people were influenced by their social environments and that these environments could differ markedly.[13] However, our knowledge of human nature continued to grow, and at the end of the twentieth century, a number of studies challenged this view. It became apparent that humans do have common characteristics. In contrast to the earlier studies that noted how different societies are to one another, evolutionary psychologists began to identify many similarities. Researchers also started to compare humans to other animals, and found that we have specific ways of acting that differentiate us from them.

Evolutionary psychologists argue that humans do have unique characteristics that evolved over a long period in response to the environments our ancestors lived in. Early humans lived in tribal groups in harsh natural environments and faced similar problems. These problems included attracting mates, acquiring resources, relationship management, the pursuit of status, and defence of the individual and the group to which they belonged. They had to understand themselves and those they interacted with. They learned to develop relations based on reciprocity and how to exercise their power.[14] Those humans whose biological structure enabled them to address these problems successfully passed their genes to the next generation. As a consequence, today's humans have brain wiring with characteristics that all humans share. We inherited many behaviours and traits of humans which are universally shared by all people.

It is not just the evolutionary psychologists who advance the idea of 'human nature'. Anthropologists discovered significant flaws in the early studies, including those of Margaret Mead. This led to more sophisticated research techniques among anthropologists, who also began to recognize human commonalities with a distinct human nature.[15] When humans regularly display traits or behaviours in different cultures at different times, it suggests that universal behaviours exist that cannot be attributed to culture. This means

13 Markoczy, L. (2003). 'In Defence of Human Nature: A Review of Managing the Human Animal'. *British Journal of Management*, 14, 376–80.
14 Kenrick, D., Li, N. and Butner, J. (2003). 'Dynamical Evolutionary Psychology: Individual Decision Rules and Emergent Social Norms'. *Psychological Review*, 110, 3–28.
15 Vredenburgh, D.J. and Shea-Van Fossen, R.J. (2010). 'Human Nature, Organizational Politics, and Human Resources Development'. *Human Resources Development Review*, 9(1), 26–47.

that evolutionary processes and genetic predispositions have caused those behavioural patterns.

We now have enough knowledge to recognize patterns of behaviour that are universally recognized as characteristic of humans. Drawing on the work of earlier researchers, Vredenburgh and Shea-Van Fossen (2010) presented a set of universal behaviours and traits found in almost 400 historical and current societies, as shown in Table 1.1. Not all of these universals are genetic in origin, as some are a result of the interplay between genetics and culture.

Table 1.1   Select human universals

Adornment	Inequality	Positive and negative
Adultery	In-group bias	reciprocity prediction and
Ascribed and achieved status	Incest regulation	planning
Children's play	Inner states of thought and	Pride
Coalitions	emotion	Property
Conflict	Jealousy	Psychosis and neurosis
Courtship	Juvenile delinquency	Resistance to domination
Coyness	Language	Risk-taking
Dance	Leadership	Rituals
Discrepancies among speech,	Loyalty	Roles
thought and action	Male activities excluding	Rules
Domineering individuals	females	Self-deception
Empathy	Male dominance in politics	Self versus other
Envy	Manipulation	Senility
Ethnocentrism	Materialism	Sexual attraction
Facial communication	Marriage	Sexual division of labour
Family	Myths	Socialization
Flirting	Names and taxonomies	Suicide
Games of skill and chance	Obligations to give and	Supernatural
Gossip	receive	Taboos
Homicide	Persons who pretend to cure	Time rhythms and cycles
Homosexuality	the ill	

Source: Data from D.J. Vredenburgh, and R.J. Shea-Van Fossen (2010). 'Human Nature, Organizational Politics, and Human Resources Development'. *Human Resources Development Review, 9(1)*, 26–47.

People share a number of things in common. In fact, Brown (1991) talks of the 'universal person', who, regardless of their culture and time, will do a number of things.[16] The universal person will use language and non-verbal expression to communicate. They are moved by sexual attraction and may get jealous.

---

16 Brown, D.E. (1991). *Human Universals*. New York: McGraw-Hill.

They have childhood fears, and can overcome their fears over time. The universal person makes tools, and uses fire to cook. Tools and fire make people feel more comfortable and secure. They also have other ways to make themselves feel better. They use stimulants, narcotics and intoxicants to change their moods or feelings.

The universal person lives part of their lives, if not all of it, with other people. Although social, they have a sense of themselves as distinct from others. Their social relations have certain characteristics. They are also aware of prestige, and members of their society are not economically equal. Their social lives are characterized by the concept of reciprocity. They reciprocate in trade and gift-giving. They also have negative reciprocity, with revenge, and if harmed, will often seek redress. Conflict is common among humans – more common than is desirable.

Many of the universal characteristics of humans described by Brown are culturally driven. For example in the West, we no longer cook by fires. For some of his categories there is a mix of culture and biology, and at times it is hard to distinguish the cultural from the biological. Nevertheless, Brown believes there can no doubt that: 'Whatever the motive may be for resisting the idea there is a human nature whose features shape culture and society, its intellectual foundations have all but collapsed. Behavioralism and the tabula rasa view of the mind are dead in the water.'[17]

Human Nature and the Brain

Another science that has offered much to this growth of knowledge is neuro-psychology. Studies of the brain have revealed much about our nature. We have learned that when chemicals such as alcohol, LSD or Prozac enter the brain, they alter our perception and emotions, and modify our behaviour. Similarly, when electric currents are sent into the brain, they alter our experiences. Brain damage can result in significant personality changes, and we can identify what parts of the brain are linked to different behaviours. We are now in no doubt that the brain is the seat of behaviour and human nature.

The biology of our brains holds many secrets about the nature of human behaviour. Consequently, it is necessary to have a basic understanding of brain structure. The first thing to note is that the human brain has some concepts

---

17 Ibid., p. 144.

that are found in other animals. The most primitive part is the brainstem, which sits at the top of the spinal cord. The brainstem does not have the capacity to think or learn, but regulates those parts of the body necessary to keep animals alive. It regulates organ metabolism and controls basic reactions and movements, and its existence is shared by all animals with more than a minimal nervous system. In the days when the world was dominated by reptiles, this form of brain would have been found in most animals. It is often called the 'reptilian brain'.

Over time, as animals evolved, the brain acquired more structures that increased its complexity. Some animals were born with mutations to their brainstem, some of which helped them survive. These mutations added layers to the brain that enabled them to perform more complicated functions. By the time the first mammals appeared, these additional layers had resulted in a new section of the brain that we now call the limbic system. This new part of the brain added emotions to the behavioural repertoire. This part of the brain generates emotions that help us survive certain threats in the environment. It is our fight or flight mechanism, and generates emotions like anger and sexual pleasure. This part of the brain is the source of those emotions the Greek philosophers called 'the passions' – and consistent with the ancient Greek view, we do share this structure with other animals.

Over time, the limbic system acquired two new capabilities: learning and memory. This helped animals to survive, as they could now learn and remember where dangers in their environment lay. The link between emotions and memory is very important for survival. Consider a tribe arriving at tree whose fruit were poisonous. Past learning would generate negative emotions regarding that fruit. If those emotions were recalled when the fruit was once again encountered, it could increase survival rates for the tribe.

The brains of mammals continued to acquire additional layers and expand their ability to survive in their environment. About 100 million years ago, a new section appeared that gave mammals an extraordinary intellectual edge. This was the neo-cortex: the seat of thought. This biological structure enabled mammals to more fully comprehend what their senses perceived in the environment. It enabled them to make better decisions leading to survival. With the neo-cortex, the higher mammals had a brain of substantially more analytical capacity than the lower animals. The benefits of a well-developed neo-cortex are supported by studies of animals like dogs and primates, which show significant intellectual capacity.

Those species with a well-developed neo-cortex have a tendency to live in social groups, and this is a pointer to a defining aspect of human nature: we are highly social. So strong is the link between the neo-cortex and socialization that the neo-cortex is often called 'the social brain'. Any species whose members can co-operate with others gains a huge advantage in the battle to survive. If we have a brain that allows us to co-operate with others, we can co-ordinate our actions when it comes to hunting for food and defending our territories. This co-ordination required humans to have the ability to communicate and conceptualize – features that occur in the neo-cortex. It is in these facilities where humans are distinctive.

Two significant features of our brain differentiate us from other primates. First is the Broca speech centre, an important part of the brain that other primates do not have. This is the part of the brain where language is focused, and in improving communication, provides a significant advantage for social co-operation.

A second difference is the slow growth rate of the human brain. For example, it only takes two years for the brain of a lemur to mature after birth; it takes six or seven years for monkeys and other apes, but the human brain takes twenty years to mature.[18] This longer period of growth enables the brain to produce more neurons – a basic unit of the brain – and this expands our capabilities to learn and memorize.[19] Studies of animal species show a strong link between brain size and the length of time required for brain development. They conclude that 'large brains and delayed development are necessary to succeed in complex societies'.[20]

The longer period it takes for our brains to develop is important in order to master the sophisticated living patterns of humans. Compared to chimpanzees, which mostly eat food that is relatively easy to access, humans acquire food in much more sophisticated ways. Young humans must learn to hunt, collect difficult-to-obtain roots and tubers, and master the sophisticated interaction that comes with such activities.[21] Most other species at the age of seven are finding sustenance, mating and protecting their own young, but human seven-year-olds are still learning.

18 Roth, G. (2003). 'Is the Human Brain Unique?', in M. Brune, H. Ribbert and W. Schiefenhovel (eds), *The Social Brain: Evolution and Pathology*, Chichester: John Wiley and Sons, pp. 29–42.
19 Ibid.
20 Bjorklund, D. and Bering, J. (2003). 'Big Brains, Slow Development and Social Complexity: The Development and Evolutionary Origins of Social Cognition', in M. Brune, H. Ribbert and W. Schiefenhovel (eds.), *The Social Brain: Evolution and Pathology*, Chichester: John Wiley and Sons, pp. 113–52.
21 Ibid.

Our large, slow-developing brains with superior communication capabilities give humans significant mental powers. We have an ability to learn and co-operate with others. However, our brain is not without flaws. The different parts of the brain do not always work in unison. Our primitive limbic system produces emotions that our neo-cortex can have trouble controlling. In fact, the limbic system often responds faster than our neo-cortex, and that means our first response is often emotional, and once aroused, emotions can take some time to subside. This means our rational response may take some time to reveal itself.

Brain biology has also been linked to whether humans are good or bad. To first understand this link, consider the high number of crimes that are committed under the influence of alcohol and drugs – chemicals that have a significant impact on brain functioning. It has been revealed that approximately half of all violent crimes are committed by people under the influence of alcohol.[22]

Psychiatrist Laurence Tancredi believes there is a close link between the brain and human morality.[23] He believes that much immoral behaviour occurs because of abnormalities in the brain. He notes that the brain is our seat of self-control, so abnormalities can reduce our ability to control our behaviour. Tancredi does not believe that *all* immoral behaviour is caused by abnormalities, but in many cases, the biological disruptions overpower those parts of the brain where rational thinking occurs.

So what does all this mean for human nature, and which of the philosophers are right? Should managers follow Theory X or Theory Y? There is an element of truth in the words of those philosophers who claimed that we are selfish. We retain our basic instincts and selfish motives for resources, sex and status. However, our neo-cortex gives us some ability to control these, but it is not always effective. There is an animal brain inside us that raises aggression and motivates us to meet our personal needs.

Plato was right: humans can find it hard to act virtuously, especially when it comes to controlling sexual desires. Our brain biology has substantial limits. Humans experience emotional outbursts, mediocre memories and momentary lapses of reason, and our brain has definite limitations in how it processes information. In fact, at times it lets us down and we goof.

---

22 Anderson C.A. and Bushman, B.J. (1997). 'External Validity of Trivial Experiments: The Case of Laboratory Aggression'. *Review of General Psychology*, 1, 19–41.
23 Tancredi, L.R. (2005). *Hardwired Behavior: What Neuroscience Reveals about Morality*, New York: Cambridge University Press.

Clearly, the distinctive feature of humans when compared to other animals is our brain's ability to communicate and conceptualize in a manner that enhances social activity. This means that Socrates is clearly right: we are social animals. In fact, it is because of our neo-cortex that you are able to be a manager and work co-operatively in organizations. Our social ability is our greatest competitive advantage, and this highlights the importance of relationship management – a key component of this book.

There is no greater example of humans' distinct nature than the organizations that characterize the modern economy. But it is also important to remember that our brains were not designed for a world of computers and corporations. The brain is not a logically structured organ, but a dynamic arena of biochemical processes that, through experience, have proven effective, mainly in times of tribal living and harsh natural environments.[24] As Daniel Goleman states in his book *Emotional Intelligence*:

> *what we are born with is what worked best for the last 50,000 generations, not the last 500 generations- and certainly not the last five. The slow deliberate forces of evolution that have shaped our emotions have done their work over the course of a million years: the last 10,000 years – despite having witnesses the rapid rise of human civilization and the explosion of the human population from 5 million to 5 billion – have left little imprint on our biological templates for emotional life ....*[25]

Earlier in this chapter, we defined human nature as 'consistent patterns of behaviour of the human species'. Psychologists now accept that many forms of social behaviour have a hard-wired or genetic foundation, such as language.[26] However, our actions are not just a result of biology. Environmental effects, including upbringing, socialization and situational factors, are also important. And this raises an important limitation of the concept of 'human nature': non-human factors can have a significant impact on our behaviour. So when we define human nature, we must define it broadly, knowing that what aspects of our nature reveal themselves are determined not just by biology, but by other features, including upbringing and environmental factors.

24 Edelman, G. (2004). *Wider than the Sky: The Phenomenal Gift of Consciousness*, New Haven, CT: Yale University Press.
25 Goleman, D. (1996). *Emotional Intelligence*, London: Bloomsbury.
26 Messick, D.M. (2004). 'Human Nature and Business Ethics', in R.E. Freeman (ed.), *Business, Science and Ethics*, Charlottesville, VA: Business Ethics Society, University of Virginia, pp. 129–33.

Our nature is seen in the things we do, and it is clear that humans are capable of a wide range of behavioural patterns. We can be truthful and dishonest, cruel and kind, lazy and hard-working. Our workers can fit both Theory X and Theory Y. Humans are capable of the worst atrocities, and history shows regular occurrences of rape, murder and genocide. However, we are also capable of great acts of kindness. It is not unusual for humans to help people they do not know, and in some cases, risk their own lives in the process.

The Concept of Human Nature and Management

In recent years, there has still been resistance to the application of evolutionary psychology and the concept of human nature to management.[27] It was resisted by those who argued that we have free will that transcends any inherited biological drives or structures. Other resisted it because they believed that our behaviours have become so sophisticated that we are no longer anchored by our biological identity. Our natural behaviours are modified by the huge array of social options available to us.

Some views of human nature are opposed for political reasons. Some feminists dislike research that argues that women and men have genetic differences that result in different workplace outcomes. For example, one study conducted by Browne (1998) argued that mammalian mothers do not like to be separated from their young.[28] As a consequence, women will generally be less likely to pursue jobs that involve longer hours, require travel and require a single-minded commitment to a career than men will. Consequently, women earn lower incomes and are less likely to be promoted by employers seeking strong commitment. Browne argues that this explains why women earn less than men. However, feminists focusing on discrimination will not welcome such explanations.

Finally, any influence of evolutionary psychology may be opposed on religious grounds. Those who believe in creation may oppose a position born of evolutionary theory. This is a genuine concern given that in a Gallup poll, 45 per cent of Americans rejected Darwin, 'and believe that God created human

---

27 Nicholson, N. and Wright, R. (2006). 'Darwinism: A New Paradigm for Organizational Behavior?'. *Journal of Organizational Behavior*, 27, 111–19.
28 Browne, K.R. (1998). 'An Evolutionary Account of Women's Workplace Status'. *Managerial and Decision Economics*, 19, 427–40.

beings pretty much in their present form about 10,000 years ago'.[29] However, creationists need not see the concept of human nature as a threat, as it can be detached from evolutionary theory.

To detach brain structure from evolutionary theory, we need only ask: what are the behaviour repertoires that God created 10,000 years ago? What characteristics would someone living in Abraham's nomadic tribe have needed to survive? Abraham's tribe had to face the same problems of attracting mates, acquiring resources, relationship management, the pursuit of status, and defence. The characteristics of the nomadic tribes that evolutionary psychologists talk of are the same as those of the tribe led by Abraham. It is only necessary to consider the structure of the brain as it is, without the evolutionary explanation.

Despite these areas of resistance, a number of attempts have been made to link management with human nature. We previously mentioned McGregor's Theory X and Theory Y. Lawrence and Nohria have also created a text embedded in core human concepts.[30] They argue that human motivations can fit in to four categories: the drive to bond, the drive to defend, the drive to learn and the drive to acquire. These drives originate in our evolutionary biology.

Nicholson has drawn on human nature to inform management practice in his book *Executive Instinct*.[31] He argues that many of the problems of modern organizational life can be linked to a poor fit between our true nature and the economic demands of modern organizations. The problem for managers is that today's environment is very different to the one in which our nature evolved. Our human nature was moulded over some four million years in which we lived in small hunter-gatherer tribes. The advent of agriculture 10,000 years ago required a new set of behaviours, while modern industrial society is different yet again. Nicolson draws on evolutionary theory to explore the importance of gossip in the workplace, how to identify leaders, the different things that men and women want from organizations, decision-making traps and the problems that occur when we manage against the grain of human nature.

---

29 Nicholson and Wright (2006).
30 Lawrence, P.R. and Nohria, N. (2002). *How Human Nature Shapes Our Choices*, San Francisco, CA: Jossey-Bass.
31 Nicholson, N. (2000). *Executive Instinct: Managing the Human Animal in the Information Age*, New York: Crown Business.

A similar position is taken by Bernhard and Glantz in their book *Staying Human in the Organization*.[32] They argue that there is a universal human nature genetically encoded from our time as hunter-gatherers. However, modern organizations are very different from the environment in which our nature was shaped, so if we are to have a happier workforce, organizations should try to more closely replicate the tribal structure, including getting rid of hierarchies. However, this ignores the fact that even in tribes, hierarchies exist. It also reflects the naturalistic fallacy that 'what happens in nature is right' – a position which might not be tenable given many of the advances in knowledge we have made.

A common theme of these books is that understanding how humans behave in organizations is best studied if we draw on recent work in human biology, ethnology, anthropology and psychology.[33] There can be no doubt that management would be enriched if built on a better perception of human nature, but I would go further and say that human nature is of importance not just to management, but to everyone working in the social sciences. In fact, it could be argued that human nature (and interpersonal relationships) should be a core subject for every university degree.

A Simple Model of Human Nature – an Oxymoron?

With the exception of the few examples mentioned above, management academics rarely approach the concept of human nature – a strange oversight given that humans are the principle resource that we manage. Of course, characteristics of humans are embedded in all management courses. These courses reveal the complexity of human behaviour, which suggests that to present a simple model may be counterproductive and an over-simplification of human behaviour and theory. However, Chapter 2 will offer a simple model detailing characteristics that managers frequently encounter in the workplace.

The sheer complexity of human behaviour and the variability in behaviours in different environments suggests a need for caution. However, there is a lot of value in using a simplified model. Although our model includes a limited number of human characteristics, this limited approach can actually help to make management education more practical and more relevant. Instead of

---

32 Bernhard, J.G. and Glantz, K. (eds) (1992). *Staying Human in the Organization: Our Biological Heritage and the Workplace*, Westport, CT: Praeger.
33 Markoczy (2003).

providing a large number of theories for management trainees to learn, we focus on a small number of theories, then link them to common workplace situations, the emphasis being on applying those theories. The irony is that by simplifying human nature, it is possible to gain a more complex understanding of workplace problems.

This approach is based on the Elaboration Theory of Learning. This theory states that learning should start with a few simple and fundamental ideas with strong practical application. These make it easier for trainees to identify with the new knowledge. Then as learning progresses, instruction becomes more complicated, elaborating on the earlier model. This method of learning draws on studies of human cognition that show that the mental models learners possess provide the scaffolding for future learning.[34] The mental model acts as an organizing device that enables learners to make sense of new knowledge.[35] This increases the ability to incorporate, integrate and assimilate more detailed information later on.[36]

The other advantage of a simplified model is that it allows us to see how different aspects of human nature affect each other. For example, when motivation is taught separately to emotion, we do not get to see how the two concepts affect each other in the workplace. In reality, emotions have a very close relationship with motivation. To give a simple example, when our motivation for self-esteem is affected by someone who insults us, this gives rise to the emotion of anger. This book argues that understanding this inter-relationship in various real-world situations is important for the development of good managers.

The simple model of human nature in Chapter 2 covers a range of characteristics of humans that contribute to a large range of workplace problems. It considers what motivates humans, what are common characteristics about the way they think, and what role emotions play. As the book progresses, we will draw on these characteristics to help explain workplace problems managers will face throughout their career.

34 Anderson, R.C., Spiro, R.J. and Anderson, M.C. (1978). 'Schemata as Scaffolding for the Representation of Information in Connected Discourse'. *American Educational Research Journal*, 15, 433–40.
35 Wilson, B. and Cole, P. (1992). 'A Critical Review of Elaboration Theory'. *Educational Technology Research and Development*, 40(3), 63–79.
36 Reigeluth, C. and Stein, S.F. (1983). 'The Elaboration Theory of Instruction', in C.M. Reigeluth (ed.), *Instructional Design Theories and Models: An Overview of their Current Status*, Hillsdale, NJ and London: Lawrence Erlbaum, pp. 335–81.

Chapter 3 considers the role of relationships in the workplace, along with methods of managing relationships to enhance productivity, and Chapter 4 then calls for constructive management that mitigates human limitations. Following this, Chapters 5, 6 and 7 explore aspects of human nature and relationships in greater depth. Throughout the book, we see how managers must constantly perform balancing acts between conflicting forces that exist at any given time. Finally, Chapter 8 looks at how human characteristics may be undermining ethical behaviour, and suggests that if we want to make the world a better place, we should focus less on social responsibility and more on being better managers:

Understanding humans is hard; so is understanding groups of humans, such as organizations. But just because something is hard, and just because anything resembling complete success is unattainable for a long way off doesn't mean that it isn't worth trying.[37]

37 Markoczy, L. and Goldberg, J. (1998). 'Management Organization and Human Nature: An Introduction'. *Managerial and Decision Economics*, 19(7–8), 387–409, p. 387.

2

Technical Specifications of the Human Resource: A Simple Model of Human Nature

The concept of human nature suggests that all humans have characteristics in common. If managers can understand those characteristics, they can become more effective. However, human nature is diverse, so we must decide what characteristics best inform management. For example, humans have so many cognitive limitations that we cannot possibly include all of them in our model. Ideally, the features we choose should be those that are most relevant to managers, organizations and social functioning.

Herein lies the first problem: every academic and manager will have their own idea about what characteristics should be included, in which case a model will never be found that satisfies everyone. We will have to settle on those characteristics that cover a wide enough range of workplace situations to enhance management training.

Cognition	Motivation	Emotion
Limited span of judgement	Understanding and control	Emotional leakages
Schemas	Self-identity	Temperament
Cognitive dissonance	Self-esteem	Gut feeling
Attribution Theory	Belonging	Limbic hijack
Reciprocity	Security	Lingering and simmering
Social Comparison Theory	Physiological	Displaced aggression
	Acquired needs	

Figure 2.1   Simple model of human nature

The model proposed in this chapter considers what motivates humans, what are common characteristics about the way they think, and what role emotions play. Figure 2.1 lists these three categories and the characteristics. As the book progresses, we will draw on these characteristics to help to explain workplace problems that managers will face throughout their careers.

Cognition

Chapter 1 revealed that the human brain has limitations – we goof. Cognitive psychology is the study of how the mind thinks and processes information. This section details some cognitive biases and patterns that can have an impact on management and worker behaviour.

LIMITED SPAN OF JUDGEMENT

An early psychological paper which revealed the mental limits of humans was written by George Miller of Harvard University.[1] Miller reviewed a number of studies, and found that the accuracy of our memory and judgement vary depending on the amount of information we have to deal with. The tasks in his studies were simple: for example, they examined how many different tones of music subjects could identify. Despite their simplicity, they revealed that we humans have an upper limit on our ability to process and remember information accurately. The upper limit varied depending on the experiment, but performance could be perfect when faced with up to five to six items. However, when given one more piece of information, performance dropped – hence Miller's title for his paper, 'The Magical Number Seven, Plus or Minus Two'.

More recent studies reveal that the upper limit is dependent on the complexity of the information, the context in which it is given, and how well we know the information. These findings have great relevance for managers who are constantly bombarded with problems, ideas and information. If judgement drops when we have too many things on our minds, we can expect highly intelligent and well-intentioned people to make bad decisions. You may be a great manager when you have three or four problems to deal with, but one more problem makes your mind go foggy.

---

1   Miller, G. (1956). 'The Magical Number Seven, Plus or Minus Two: Some Limits on our Capacity for Processing Information'. *Psychological Review*, 63, 81–97.

The situation is particularly bad when we are dealing with a new issue and are bombarded with information. We feel overloaded and have difficulty making sense of the information. Our decision-making is slow, and we are in danger of appearing wishy-washy to our staff. We can all experience such moments of overload.

Awareness of your limitations as a manager is vital to avoid making mistakes. It is important to recognize when you may be operating under conditions that impede your performance. Reaching the limit of your span of judgement can have a significant impact on your effectiveness as a manager. It also raises the importance of organizing your thoughts and finding decision-making tools that help to increase the amount of information you can process effectively. Delegation can relieve much of the pressure, but you have to be careful that you do not merely shift the overload to your staff, as they too will have limited spans of judgement.

When writing books and articles, I feel this aspect of human nature is the most important to acknowledge if I am to increase my output. When writing, I frequently have so much research material that I don't know where to start. I have learned that the most important part of my work is organizing my thoughts before I write a single word. I then deal with each subject in the book individually, breaking the information down in to smaller units of information that are easier to process. Recognizing my cognitive limitations was an important feature that dramatically expanded my production.

SCHEMAS

We may be born with instincts and drives, but there is a distinct limit on the knowledge we possess at birth. When we are first introduced to a topic, our knowledge is very rudimentary, but over time we gain more experience and knowledge. Through this process, we build mental frameworks about how the world works. These mental models are called *schemas*. Schemas are created as we grow and gain knowledge. To that extent, our schemas are reflections of our life experience, and because people have different life experiences, they will have different schemas. This can be both an advantage and a disadvantage in the workplace.

It can be a disadvantage as it can be a source of conflict. People with different views will disagree over how to perceive certain issues and how to solve them. These views can be strongly held, as they are backed up by years of experience and learning. It could be said that when managing staff, you are actually managing a collection of diverse life experiences. Much of your time can be spent reconciling those differences. However, this can also be an advantage, in that different world views can strengthen the experience and knowledge base you can draw on at work.

No one can have life experiences that replicate those of all other people. Of course, this includes you, the manager, and like your staff, you may find yourself in conflict with those holding different schemas. Like every other human, your views will be shaped by your own personal life experiences. It is another reminder to acknowledge your limitations if you are to maximize your performance.

Because of the limit of our life experiences, our mental views are imprecise, partial and idiosyncratic.[2] However, the fact they are based on years of experience gives the views strong credence for each individual. To tell someone they are wrong is to deny the validity of their life experience. This raises the importance of recognizing and respecting the existing schemas that staff hold when they impact on work, particularly when dealing with conflict and staff training. We need to understand how a person views a topic before attempting to address it. Once we understand their existing schema, we can shape our conflict-resolution or tuition more effectively.

Schemas are also important for understanding a worker's ability to learn. If we understand the schemas our staff hold, we can tailor our training so it is less likely to encounter resistance. However, sometimes our beliefs are so entrenched that we cannot easily alter them, and we may not be prepared to change. After all, our mental models are based on a lifetime of learning. The difference between the new information and the old thoughts can create *cognitive dissonance* (see below). We often dispute that information and go through denial. This can create a problem in the workplace.

COGNITIVE DISSONANCE

A common cognitive limitation occurs when we experience cognitive dissonance, where we have two thoughts in our head which are not compatible. This psychological phenomenon was discovered in the 1950s by Leon Festinger, who conducted an experiment in which he asked subjects to do tedious tasks

---

2   Driscoll, M. (1994). *Psychology of Learning for Instruction*. Boston, MA: Allyn and Bacon.

such as placing pegs into a board.[3] Some of the subjects were paid $20, while some were paid only $1. Festinger was surprised to discover that those being paid well reported being bored with the job, while those only paid $1 reported that the task was fun. Why was that?

Festinger discovered an interesting psychological phenomenon. It seems that people did not want to admit they had wasted their time, so they compensated psychologically by convincing themselves that the task was enjoyable. This finding has been supported by a large number of studies which show that if confronted with bad information, humans distort the information to make themselves feel happier. We do not do it consciously, but this subconscious deception leaves us in a happier state of mind.

Cognitive dissonance has been linked to hypocrisy.[4] For example, you believe something, but find yourself doing something against your beliefs. There is a dissonance between your actions and your beliefs. To avoid feeling like a hypocrite, you must act to avoid the discomfort. This can motivate us to improve, but it can also lead to managerial self-deception – something we will explore later in this book.

ATTRIBUTION THEORY

Attribution Theory refers to where we attribute the cause of an action. For example, if we are harmed by a colleague, do we assume they did it on purpose, or do we accept that there were extenuating circumstances? If we assume they did it on purpose, we are making an internal attribution, but if we assume that they were affected by circumstances, we are making an external attribution.

As a manager, you will regularly have to attribute the cause of behaviour, with important consequences if you get it wrong. For example, is the cause of your worker's poor performance laziness, or detrimental circumstances they are going through? Unfortunately, psychologists have discovered that we can fall into cognitive traps when making attributions. The first is the *fundamental attribution error* – when making judgements about the behaviour of other people, we have a tendency to underestimate the influence of external factors

---

3   Festinger, L. and Carlsmith, J.M. (1959). 'Cognitive Consequences of Forced Compliance'. *Journal of Abnormal and Social Psychology*, 58(2), 203–10.
4   Reeve, J.M. (2004). *Understanding Motivation and Emotion*, 4th edn, Hoboken, NJ: Wiley.

and overestimate the influence of internal or personal factors. This makes it easier to blame someone for a mistake.

The second cognitive trap is *self-serving bias*, which refers to attributing the cause of our own behaviour. We have a tendency to attribute our successes to internal factors such as our ability; however, if we fail, we blame external factors such as luck or fate.

RECIPROCITY

Reciprocity is the tendency to treat others as they have treated us. It is a core component of interpersonal relations in all societies. In Maori society, it is referred to as *utu*. In China, it is linked to the philosopher Confucius, who was once asked, 'Is there one word which may serve as a rule of practice for all one's life?' He answered, 'Is not reciprocity such a word? What you do not want done to yourself, do not do to others.'

In Western society, reciprocity is embodied in statements from the Bible or Torah such as 'an eye for an eye', and in the words of Jesus, 'do unto others as you would have them do to you'. While these comments recognize an underlying human principle, they also reveal important differences. The comment 'eye for an eye' says that you can do bad things to people who do bad things to you. However, Confucius stresses that we should not do anything bad to other people, while Jesus goes one step further and says that we should actually do good to people. Behind all these different interpretations is the idea that we should treat people as they treat us (or want them to treat us).

Despite these differences in interpretation, reciprocity remains a powerful notion for guiding workplace interaction. Reciprocity can occur at a number of levels in the workplace. A worker will perceive their relationship with the organization in terms of reciprocity. If the worker feels that the organization offers good job conditions such as pay, promotion, job security, esteem and emotional support, the worker is likely to reciprocate with greater emotional attachment and commitment to the workplace. The worker feels more obligated to help the organization to achieve its goals.[5] This results in a higher-quality relationship between the worker and organization.

---

5   Ladebo, O.J., Adamu, C.O. and Olaoye, O.J. (2005). 'Relative Contributions of Perceived Organizational Support and Organizational Justice to Extension Personnel's Job Satisfaction'. *Journal of International Agricultural and Extension Education*, 12(1), 65–75; Rhoades, L. and

Reciprocity is also important between the worker and supervisor. When supervisors devote more time, resources, advice and trust, an employee feels obliged to reciprocate. The result is a high-quality work relationship which is sustained into the future.[6] Reciprocity is also a feature of relationships between work colleagues, as we will discuss later in this book.

SOCIAL COMPARISON THEORY

Another common cognitive phenomenon which humans use to gauge fairness is social comparison: we compare our own situation with others, and if there is a discrepancy, we feel less happy. It is only natural that we look to others to make comparisons, as they provide ready measuring sticks.

A number of researchers have found examples of social comparison in the workplace, including Vecchio, who in 1984 suggested that workers make comparisons with others they work with. Workers are very sensitive to issues of equity and where they stand in the workplace.[7] Perhaps the most famous study is one in which workers were asked if they would like to earn an extra £2, but their total pay would be less than people in a nearby department. Alternatively, they could earn only £1 extra, but their total pay would be more than their colleagues'. The results showed that the workers preferred to earn the smaller amount.[8] They were more interested in how their pay compared to their colleagues' than the total amount they earned.

The management theory most closely based on social comparison is Adam's Equity Theory, which states that workers compare what they get out of a job (outputs) and what they put into a job (such as skills, qualifications), then compare this to the outputs and inputs of their colleagues. They don't mind if a colleague is paid more if that worker puts more into the job, but if their inputs are not proportionally higher, they will feel dissatisfied.

Eisenberger, R. (2002). 'Perceived Organizational Support: A Review of the Literature'. *Journal of Applied Psychology*, 87(4), 698–714.

6   Brandes, P., Dharwadkar, R. and Wheatley, K. (2004). 'Social Exchanges within Organizations and Work Outcomes: The Importance of Local and Global Relationships'. *Group & Organizational Management*, 29(3), 276–301; Vandenberghe, C., Bentein, K. and Stinglhamber, F. (2004). 'Affective Commitment to the Organization, Supervisor, and Work Group: Antecedents and Outcomes'. *Journal of Vocational Behavior*, 64(1), 47–71.

7   Vecchio, R.P. (1984). 'Models of Psychological Inequality'. *Organizational Behavior and Human Performance*, 34, 266–82.

8   Brown, R.J. (1978). 'Divided We Fall: An Analysis of Relations between Sections of a Factory Work-force', in H. Tajfel (ed.), *Differentiation Between Social Groups*, London: Academic Press, pp. 395–429.

Motivation

The second group of human characteristics covered in our model refers to human motivation. Most management textbooks view motivation as a tool for increasing worker effort. It is an approach embodied in the Hawthorne studies, the Job Characteristics Model and Adam's Equity Theory. However, this book views motivation differently. When we use motivation to understand human nature, we consider how core motivation affects *all* behaviour in the workplace, not just how hard people work.

The problem is deciding what motives to include in our model, particularly given that researchers cannot even agree among themselves. For example, McClelland (1958) argues that we are motivated by achievement, power and affiliation.[9] However, Glass (1998) argues that we are driven by a drive for territory, dominance, sexuality and reproduction.[10] To make matters worse, different workers will be motivated by different factors, and what motivates them at one point in time may not motivate them at a later date.

The most common motivation model in use at business schools is Maslow's Hierarchy of Needs. However, one of the motives he identifies, self-actualization, is a concept that can blur practical use, and would be of greater utility if broken down further. Maslow (1943) described actualization as: 'the desire for self-fulfillment, namely the tendency for him [the individual] to become actualized in what he is potentially. This tendency might be phrased as the desire to become more and more what one is, to become everything that one is capable of becoming.'[11]

The problem with actualization is the broadness of its description. To draw up a list which lends itself better to application in the workplace, we will adapt Maslow's simple model by replacing self-actualization with two concepts: the first is *a motive for self-identity*, and the second is *a motive to control and understand our environment*. Both of these will be expanded on below. Given the desire to provide a simple model with a high practical component, we use the following list of human core motivations:

---

9   McClelland, D.C. (1958). 'Methods of Measuring Human Motivation', in J.W. Atkinson (ed.), *Motives in Fantasy, Action and Society*, Princeton, NJ: D. Van Nostrand, pp. 12–13.
10 Glass, J. (1998). *The Animal within Us: Lessons from Our Animal Ancestors*, Corona del Mar, CA: Donington Press.
11 Maslow, A.H. (1943). 'A Theory of Human Motivation'. *Psychological Review*, 50, 370–96.

- understanding and control;

- self-identity;

- social belonging;

- self-esteem;

- security;

- acquired needs and sensual pleasure;

- physiological factors such as sex, thirst, hunger and fundamentals of regulation.

The list above includes physiological motives. At first glance, these appear to have little relevance for managers, but this is not correct. A staff member whose basic physiological needs are not met will not enjoy the body functioning that enables full performance. Workers may not even recognize subtle changes in their bodies that are affecting them, and given the gradual nature of some bodily changes, this can have an impact on output. For example, a worker may not recognize declining eyesight. They just develop a tendency to skim-read. Similarly, small misalignments in the spine can sap workers' energy levels, causing them to appear lethargic or lazy. Things as simple as diet or not eating regularly during the day can affect a worker's drive and judgement, as well as affecting their relationships with colleagues. Workers can become niggly and uncooperative when their stomachs are empty.

Many of our basic needs are met not in the workplace, but as a consequence of workplace activity. Workers use their income to buy the goods that satisfy their basic needs. As each worker knows their particular needs best, most managers often limit their interest in the particular motives of each worker. However, motivation theory remains a major part of business education, and the need to recognize these idiosyncratic motives emerges in theories such as Expectancy Theory, which suggests that employers should tailor work incentives to match the individual desires of their workers.

UNDERSTANDING AND CONTROL

When our ancestors lived in tribes, the more they understood and had a sense of control of the environment in which they lived, the greater their chance of survival. Unstable environments can be much harder to negotiate, and make life decisions more difficult. Consequently, we strive to understand the world around us. We spend money on education, listen to news programmes and read widely.

Many psychological studies confirm that a sense of control makes people feel happy.[12] We do not like the inconsistency that comes from unstable and uncertain environments,[13] and are happiest in a world we understand. We like our environment to be stable and consistent with our beliefs.

This need for control is found in modern workplaces. For example, one study examined 7,400 civil servants working in London. It found that lack of control in the workplace was related to poor health. Workers who had little say in how they did their work (or with whom) had a 50 per cent higher chance of developing symptoms of coronary heart disease.[14] Those workers with more job flexibility were much less exposed to such risks, and those with little control over work demands and pressures were most exposed.

Perhaps the time when our sense of control is most under threat in the workplace is during business restructuring. This is a time when there is a fear of job losses, management changes, and wage and hiring freezes. With little sense of control, staff commonly feel an increase in anxiety, and the greater the degree of uncertainty, the greater the anxiety.[15] It is a time of emotional and mental adjustment, particularly for older workers, and it is no surprise that such changes are often met with workplace resistance and cynicism. They strike at our core needs in life: certainty and control.

---

12 Marcus, G.F. (2008). *Kluge: The Haphazard Construction of the Human Mind*, New York: Houghton Mifflin, p. 131.
13 Cooper, J. (2001). 'Motivating Cognitive Change: The Self Standards Model of Dissonance', in J. Forgas, K. Williams and L. Wheeler (eds), *The Social Mind: Cognitive and Motivational Aspects of Interpersonal Behavior*, Cambridge: Cambridge University Press, pp. 72–91.
14 Syme, L. (1997). 'Explaining Inequalities in Heart Disease'. *The Lancet*, 26 July.
15 Lopez, F.G. (1983). 'The Victims of Corporate Failure: Some Preliminary Observations'. *Personnel & Guidance Journal*, 61(10), 631–2.

SELF-IDENTITY

People have a strong desire to know who they are, their capabilities, potentialities and place in the world. We may even go to some extent to 'find ourselves', spending money on education, travel and spiritual enlightenment. As we learn more about ourselves, we develop a sense of identity. This involves discovering how we relate to society and what our personal potential is. Such knowledge about our strengths and weaknesses can help us to plan our lives and make decisions that enhance our welfare and happiness.

As we get older and gain more life experiences, we gain knowledge about ourselves and build a sense of identity. We recognize our own values, beliefs, personality traits, motives and abilities. We discover our personality traits and our idiosyncratic characteristics. However, our behaviour patterns can change depending on the situation we are in. The personality we reveal at work can be very different from the personality we reveal to our friends. With this in mind, many people in search of themselves deliberately put themselves in unusual situations to see how they respond. Diversity of experience reveals a greater breadth of behavioural patterns depending on the situation.

Our sense of identity can consist of a number of levels. In some cases, our identity is referenced by the groups we belong to. We define ourselves by the sports team we follow, our religious community, and often our workplace, particularly if we feel a strong sense of belonging to it. This opens up the possibility for alignment between personal and organizational goals. If the worker identifies with the organization, it can increase the worker's sense of community, as well as satisfying a core motive for the individual employee.[16]

In developing our sense of identity, we create what psychologists call a *self-concept*. A self-concept is a mental representation of our self.[17] It is a collection of schemas about how we perceive our self in different contexts and situations. It may include how we view our self scholastically, our athletic competence, physical appearance, peer acceptance, close friendships and romantic appeal.

Our self-concept will also include a sense of moral identity that reflects our ethical values and the extent to which these values are part of our sense

---

16 Krishnan V.R. (2005). 'Transformational Leadership and Outcomes: Role of Relationship Duration'. *Leadership and Organization*, 26(6), 442–57.
17 Markus, H. (1977). 'Self Schemata and Processing Information about the Self'. *Journal of Personality and Social Psychology*, 35, 63–8.

of identity. People vary in the extent to which moral concerns are part of their self-description,[18] but most people view themselves as moral and reasonable.[19]

Sometimes we behave in ways that make us feel stupid. This can create a gap between what we believe about our self and what we actually do, resulting in cognitive dissonance. We discover a gap between our ideal self and our real self.[20] This can motivate us to improve our behaviour, in which case, a useful capability for both you and your workers to develop is an ability to acknowledge your faults. However self-criticism is a capacity in itself that takes time to develop,[21] and it is common for people to overlook bad information about themselves.

While we devote a lot of energy to finding ourselves, our self-concept may not be accurate. Inaccuracies can be caused by lack of experience, or alternatively, a desire to protect our self. It must be remembered that the information we gain about our self helps to guide our lives. It tells us what situations to enter and what situations to avoid. If we have a positive self-concept, it gives us hope and optimism for the future. So it is not surprising that psychologists Sedikidies and Strube state: 'to be effective in coping with the world, the individual must have a positive and well protected self concept, even if that self concept is not truly accurate'.[22]

Given the psychological benefits of having a positive self-identity, it only makes sense that people should strive to maintain a positive self-view. This is confirmed by research which shows that people actively solicit feedback that confirms their desired view of themselves.[23] Information that contradicts our self-view is often dismissed as inaccurate. Studies of people's memories show similar distortions. We have a tendency to remember positive information about ourselves, but have poorer memories of situations in which we shone less brightly. However, this can make it difficult for managers who often have to break negative news to their employees.

---

18 Blasi, A. (1984). 'Moral Identity: Its Role in Moral Functioning', in W. Kurtines and J. Gewirtz (eds), *Morality, Moral Behavior and Moral Development*, New York: Wiley, pp. 128–39.
19 Reeve (2004), p. 269.
20 Markus, H. and Nurius, P. (1986). 'Possible Selves'. *American Psychologist*, 41, 954–69.
21 Hart, D. (2005). 'The Development of Moral Identity', in G. Carlo and C.P. Edwards (eds), *Moral Motivation through the Lifespan*, Lincoln, NE: University of Nebraska Press.
22 Sedikides, C.and Strube, M.J. (1997). 'Self Evaluation: To Thine Own Self Be Good, To Thine Own Self Be Sure, To Thine Own Self Be True, and To Thine Own Self Be Better'. *Advances in Experimental Social Psychology*, 29, 209–69, p. 223.
23 Ibid.

On the positive side, these cognitive tendencies are not all bad news. People have a genuine desire for self-improvement.[24] They are motivated to improve their traits, abilities and skills. Such improvements help to raise self-esteem and bring a worker closer to their ideal self. Hence, the desire for self-identity is a force that managers can use to help improve performance, if done correctly.

However, the strength of this drive for identity can vary for each worker. The search for identity can be greatest among those who are young and still in a state of discovery. It is common among those who are unhappy. To find happiness, they need to discover what their identity is so that they can make better life decisions. Business consultant Will Schutz believes that workers who 'know themselves' seem to be calmer, stronger, more real, more honest, more successful in relationships, and genuinely caring and helpful people.[25] However, this needs to be supported by research.

SOCIAL BELONGING

In the previous chapter, we revealed how our brain structure enabled humans to live in social groups and develop complex social relations, so it should come as no surprise that psychologists have found that we are motivated to belong in social relationships. Today, the human drive for connectedness is well documented. However, research has shown that it is not the number of social connections that is important for our happiness, but the quality of those connections.

This sense of belonging has historically been important for survival. For most of our existence, the human race has lived in small tribal groups. Tribal living increased the ability to gain food from co-ordinated hunts, as well as allowing for greater defensive capabilities. Those with an inner need to belong were more likely to survive and have children with the same instincts.

In the workplace, this motive for belonging can help gain increased commitment from workers as well as providing them with greater job satisfaction. If workers belong to a group where they depend on each other to achieve goals and that work group provides emotional satisfaction, members tend to exhibit greater group commitment.[26] If co-workers are accepted and

---

24 Ibid.
25 Schutz, W. (1996). 'Self Esteem at Work'. *Heart at Work*, 73–82.
26 Vandenberghe, Bentein and Stinglhamber (2004).

positively evaluated by their colleagues, they can also enjoy a higher sense of self-esteem.[27]

However, we should not assume that all workers always desire close relationships. Workers may experience satisfaction from being part of a workplace but still prefer to work by themselves. The last thing they may want is a manager who exaggerates the 'family nature' of their organization and pushes them towards workers with whom they have little compatibility. The human motive for social belonging is a powerful tool for managers, but it must be applied subtly. Most workers have a better idea of whom they get on with than any manager. Nevertheless, managers can act to improve relationships, as we will discover later in this book.

SELF-ESTEEM

When humans lived in tribal societies, status had important survival and reproductive implications. A person with high status in the tribe would have greater access to scarce and desirable resources such as food, protection and sexual partners. Those who successfully sought high status would be more likely to have offspring that survived and passed on their genes. The pursuit of status is logical, but people pursuing status may not always be consciously aware of their underlying motives:[28]

> Status and self-esteem are linked to how others perceive us. However, self-esteem is not just a question of how others perceive us, but also how we perceive ourselves. Schutz says that self-esteem: is the feeling I have about my self concept. To the degree that I experience myself as being like my ideal, and as being unlike the self I want to avoid, I have positive self esteem. Similarly, the more I fall short of my ideal, the more disappointed I am in myself.[29]

Of all our core motives, perhaps the most important for a manager to acknowledge is self-esteem. If you are to function effectively as a manager, you need to protect the self-esteem of your workers. However, in Western society, we do not pay enough attention to this. Pride has traditionally been seen as

27 Reece, B.L. and Brandt, R. (1999). *Effective Human Relations in Organizations* (7th edn), Boston, MA: Houghton Mifflin.
28 Alexander, R.D. (1990). *How Did Humans Evolve? Reflections On a Uniquely Unique Species*, Ann Arbor, MI: Ann Arbor Museum of Zoology, University of Michigan Special Publication no. 1.
29 Schutz (1996).

a sin. Despite the importance of self-esteem, Western managers are regularly accused of being too critical and not showing enough respect to their workers.

Self-esteem contributes much to personal welfare. It refers to an individual's evaluation of their own overall competence and social worth.[30] People with high self-esteem feel secure, capable, acceptable and worthy; those with low self-esteem view themselves in negative terms and have self-doubts.[31] They are also more likely to suffer from anxiety and depression.[32] This has important implications for productivity. If workers believe they have competence, it will increase their job satisfaction, commitment and performance.[33]

Consultant Will Schutz goes as far as to call self-esteem 'the key to productivity'.[34] He claims that low self-esteem builds rigidities that affect teamwork, conflict-resolution, problem-solving and other workplace functions. Finally, healthy self-esteem can help people to have a positive view of their world, including the workplace. With this in mind, Schutz suggests that productivity can be increased by enhancing workers' self-esteem. Managers can contribute to workers' sense of significance and competence, but it must be based on reality. You should not artificially boost your workers' egos, as this could lead to a number of problems. An artificial view of ability may not be sustainable, and may be counterproductive in the long term.

Ideally, we want workers with a positive but realistic assessment of their abilities, but sadly, our cognitive biases combine with our desire for self-esteem to create an illusion of overconfidence. People think they are better than they are. Research shows that people tend to perceive themselves as above average in a large range of personal characteristics. We believe we are better at driving, have higher ethical standards, work better, possess finer social and leadership skills and have better health prospects.[35] We also believe we have greater managerial adaptability. It is important to note that it is not just workers who experience these cognitive distortions, but also their managers – you.

---

30 Kreitner, R., Kinicki, A. and Buelens, M. (2002). *Organizational Behavior*, 2nd edn, Maidenhead: McGraw-Hill.

31 Ladebo, O.J., Olaoye O.J. and Adamu, C.O. (2008). 'Extension Personnel's Self-esteem and Workplace Relationships: Implications for Job Satisfaction and Affective Organizational Commitment Foci'. *The Journal of Agricultural Education and Extension*, 14(3), 249–63.

32 Alloy, L.B. and Abrahamson, L.T. (1988). 'Depressive Realism: Four Theoretical Approaches', in L.B. Alloy (ed.), *Cognitive Processes in Depression*, New York: Guilford Press, pp. 223–65.

33 Ladebo, Olaoye and Adamu (2008).

34 Schutz (1996).

35 Myers, D.G. (1998). *Psychology*, 5th edn, New York: Worth.

Leading researchers in this area are David Dunning and Justin Kruger at Cornell University. They became interested in it after reading a report about McArthur Wheeler, who attempted to rob a bank in broad daylight with no disguise. Wheeler was quickly arrested by the police, who showed him surveillance tapes that clearly identified him. Mr Wheeler looked at the tapes with disbelief, saying, 'But I wore the juice.' He was under the impression that rubbing lemon juice on his face made it undetectable by video cameras.[36]

On hearing of this robbery report, the Cornell professors discovered what is now known as the *Dunning-Kruger effect*. If people do not know what is required to be good at something, they do not know how bad they are at it. Not only did the bank robber lack the skills to be good at it, he also lacked the skills required to know his limitations. This has importance for the workplace, heightening risk as workers attempt things they shouldn't. Secondly, as many of our worst-performing staff do not have the skills to recognize how bad their performance is, you as their manager will need to inform them of their shortfalls, but will confront defensive self-esteem. They will not want to acknowledge the criticisms, or if they do, it may create a sense of disassociation from the workplace.

When people have poor insight into their abilities, they will eventually experience frustrations and disappointments in life. Being aware of this can also help staff avoid very serious workplace problems where mistakes can cause significant harm and costs to themselves and others.[37] The challenge is to eliminate or reduce such illusions while maintaining the worker's self-esteem.

Recognizing failure is an important part of the learning process, and many people lack the skills to do this. The solution to such illusions of confidence is to give people skills so that not only can they do their job, but they have the capability to assess their own performance accurately. However, overconfidence is not just a factor of poor ability; other cognitive biases can contribute to this, most importantly self-serving bias (see above).

This raises the question of whether well-educated people should be able to avoid these traps. After all, the bank robber in the example above is hardly

---

36 Smith, F. (2010). 'Delusional Conundrum', *The Press*, 18–19 September, H1.
37 Koriat, A. and Bjork, R. (2006). 'Illusions of Competence during Study Can be Remedied by Manipulations that Enhance Learners' Sensitivity to Retrieval Conditions at Test', *Memory and Cognition*, 34(5), 959–72.

typical of managers and highly skilled workers. Sadly, the research suggests that well-educated people do fall in to these traps. For example, in one study, 90 per cent of a college faculty considered themselves above-average teachers.[38] Two thirds rated themselves in the top quarter – a mathematical impossibility.

Unrealistic confidence is common in business. A study of managers found high levels of overconfidence in their firms' future growth rates, with only 25 per cent thinking their growth would be below-average.[39] A number of studies have revealed that entrepreneurs are particularly prone to exaggerate the chances their businesses will succeed.[40] Research has also found overconfidence among a very large percentage of financial officers and managers,[41] and one study actually found that overconfident managers have a higher probability of being promoted to CEO.[42]

All in all, these examples reveal that even those at the highest levels have a tendency towards overconfidence.[43] It is actually normal to have these biases, as psychologist Marta Coelho notes: 'There is evidence that normal, mentally healthy individuals' perceptions of reality are characterized not by an accurate assessment of their personal qualities, a realistic estimate of their degree of personal control, and a realistic outlook on the future, but are biased and self-serving.'[44]

However, these self-illusions may have a positive effect. They may lead people to try harder so that they do in fact succeed more often. They create a self-fulfilling prophecy, in that the excessive confidence helps to motivate people. They perceive less of a chance of failure, and this can encourage them to attempt

38 Cross, K.P. (1977). 'Not Can, but Will College Teaching be Improved?'. *New Directions for Higher Education*, 17, 1–15.
39 Larwood, L. and Whittaker, W. (1977). 'Managerial Myopia: Self Serving Biases in Organizational Planning'. *Journal of Applied Psychology*, 62(2), 194–8.
40 Cooper, A.C., Woo, C.Y. and Dunkelberg, W.C. (1988). 'Entrepreneurs' Perceived Chances for Success'. *Journal of Business Venturing*, 3(2), 97–108.
41 Russo, J.E. and Schoemaker, P.J.H. (1992). 'Managing Overconfidence'. *Sloan Management Review*, 33(2), 7–17.
42 Goel, A.M. and Thakor, A.V. (2002). 'Do Overconfident Managers Make Better Leaders?' (working paper), Chicago, IL: De Paul University.
43 Kennedy, E.J., Lawton, L. and Plumlee, E.L. (2002). 'Blissful Ignorance: The Problem of Unrecognized Incompetence and Academic Performance'. *Journal of Marketing Education*, 24(3), 243–52.
44 Coelho, M. (2010). 'Unrealistic Optimism: Still a Neglected Trait'. *Journal of Business and Psychology*, 25(3), 397–408.

things that they might not otherwise consider. It has also been linked with better health outcomes, including lower mortality rates for cancer patients.[45]

One of the main reasons we do not want to impair self-esteem is because of the psychological benefits associated with it. High self-esteem can be linked to optimism, self-efficacy and resilience. Optimism is associated with a positive outlook, and is linked with positive emotions and motivation, but unlike overconfidence, it is expected to be more realistic.[46] Self-efficacy refers to people's confidence that they can complete tasks. It requires a positive belief about themselves and the ability to get through the barriers they confront. Resilience refers to people's ability to bounce back from bad experiences and cope in the face of adversity.

In a study of manufacturing firms, Luthans (2002) found that that self-efficacy, optimism, hope and resilience were linked with higher performance and job satisfaction.[47] While there is a need for more research in this area, it seems that possession of these traits is likely to help workers weather the dynamic storms facing modern organizations. The implication is that you must treat workers' self-esteem as a resource to be managed carefully.

What we need is *realistic self-esteem* – something that you as a manager can create by setting goals and helping your staff to attain the skills to achieve them. Not only will this raise their self-esteem, but the sense of growth and achievement can enhance the link between their identity and sense of belonging in the workplace.

Emotions

Emotions leapt to prominence for managers after the publication of Daniel Goleman's book *Emotional Intelligence*. Goleman described how our brain structure and emotions are linked, and how they affect human behaviour. Emotions are seated in our limbic system. This is a very primitive part of the brain, in contrast to the neo-cortex, which is our rational social part.

---

45 Taylor, S.E., Kemeny, M.E., Aspinwall, L.G., Schneider, S.G., Rodriguez, R. and Herbert, M. (1992). 'Optimism, Coping, Psychological Distress and High-risk Sexual Behavior among Men at Risk for Acquired Immunodeficiency Syndrome (AIDS)'. *Journal of Personality and Social Psychology*, 63(3), 460–73.

46 Luthans, F. (2002). 'The Need for and Meaning of Positive Organizational Behavior'. *Journal of Organizational Behavior*, 23, 695–706.

47 Ibid.

The differences between these two brain parts are such that Goleman actually says: 'in a sense, we have two brains, two minds and two different kinds of intelligence: rational and emotional'.[48]

For early man, emotions performed a very important role in co-ordinating the brain's different functions – a role they continue to play today. For example, if we are sleeping and are suddenly attacked by a predator, our emotions take over and override our need for sleep. The priority is fight or flight, not sleep. Consequently, when psychologists define emotions, they include how emotions take over our thinking, prioritize and propel us to act. For example, Tooby and Cosmides (1990) define emotions 'as super-ordinate mental programs that "orchestrate" and prioritize the functioning of the entire set of mental programs when critical events arise'.[49] Similarly, Reeve describes emotions as 'short lived, feeling-arousal-purposive-expressive phenomena that help us adapt to the opportunities and challenges we face during life events'.[50]

Our emotions are aroused by a change in the environment. These changes trigger our limbic system to release hormones that are linked to emotion. These emotions then propel us to act. Our bodies experience physiological changes when emotion is aroused, providing bodily support for actions such as fight or flight.[51]

Emotions are triggers to action, and it is possible to pair emotions to our motivations. For example, an emotion of loneliness can be linked to our motive for belonging. Shame can be linked to self-esteem, while fear can be linked to security needs. Emotions are also linked to the achievement of goals. Our emotions are aroused when we judge, consciously or unconsciously, that progress on our current goals is threatened or requires some adjustment.[52] Emotions can clearly be linked with goals. We feel happiness for goal attainment, sadness at failure or loss, while anger is aroused when our goals are frustrated or blocked.

---

48 Goleman, D. (1995). *Emotional Intelligence*, New York: Bantam Books.
49 Tooby, J. and Cosmides, L. (1990). 'The Past Explains the Present: Emotional Adaptations and the Structure of the Ancestral Environment'. *Ethology and Sociobiology*, 11, 375–424, cited in Oatley, K., Keltner, D. and Jenkins, J.M. (2006). *Understanding Emotions*, 2nd edn, Oxford: Blackwell, p. 64.
50 Reeve (2004), 294.
51 Levenson, R.W. (1992). 'Autonomic Nervous System Differences among Emotions'. *Psychological Science*, 3, 23–7.
52 Oatley, K. and Johnson-Laird, P.N. (1987). 'Toward a Cognitive Theory of Emotions'. *Cognition and Emotion*, 1, 29–50.

There are times when the limbic system is so powerfully activated that it hijacks all other neural activity. An important part of the limbic system is the amygdala, which acts as the brain's alarm. To protect us from attack, our emotions must overpower all other mental processes within an instant and focus on the threat. The speed with which the limbic system works can cause us to quickly run from harm. For example, the fear that is aroused when a dangerous machine is broken can provide significant protection. If we wait until our neo-cortex has taken in all the information, we may lose a hand in the machine.

An emotion that evolved to protect our ancestors from attack can be excessive when aroused in the workplace. Ideally, we would like to control our emotions, but this is not always easy. In his book *Emotional Intelligence*, Goleman talks of *emotional hi-jacking*, when the limbic structure is aroused and takes over our brain. This can lead to rage or anger with little rational activity occurring in our neo-cortex. Because of the amygdala's historical role as the brain's alarm, it has the ability to override the neo-cortex. We snap into a flow of emotion. Goleman explains:

> When the amygdale hits the brain's panic button, it induces a cascade that begins with the release of a hormone known as CRF and ends with a flood of stress hormones, mainly cortisol. The hormones we secrete under stress are enough for a single bout of fight or flight – but once secreted, they stay in the body for hours, and each successive upsetting incident adds more stress hormones to the levels already there. The resulting build-up can make the amygdale a hair trigger, ready to hijack us into anger or panic at the least provocation.[53]

The build-up of cortisol can also contribute to stress. When cortisol levels are high, we make more mistakes and have trouble focusing mentally, as irrelevant thoughts intrude upon out thinking. It creates stress, which if sustained can lead to burnout.

Emotions can be positive, including joy, contentment, gratitude and love. Negative emotions include sadness, fear, anger, shame and embarrassment. Many of the great belief systems stress that we should control negative emotions: for example, Buddhism states that we should strive to reduce the big three of craving, agitation and hatred.[54] Sadly, the structure of the brain is such

---

53 Goleman, D. (1998). *Working with Emotional intelligence*, London: Bloomsbury, p. 75.
54 Reeve (2004).

that we have little or no control over when we are overcome by emotion, nor what emotion it will be.[55]

While we cannot control the activation of emotions, we can limit their effect by making an effort to stay composed, avoiding inciting situations, and developing relaxation techniques such as meditation. These are not always easy to do, but if we allow emotions to dwell and take over our thinking, it can have an effect not just on our work, but on our personal welfare.

Emotions are strongly linked to our social interactions. You can witness this merely by watching people at an airport or railway station.[56] People are happy when they meet a friend. Similarly, the airport departure lounge can be a place of many tears. Our emotions are reflected in our body language, and signal much about our underlying emotions and motivation. A smile is not just a smile; it is an invitation to a co-operative relationship. Similarly, an angry expression is a declaration of conflict.

Emotions play a key role in defining and negotiating social relations.[57] For example, anger is often aroused by a sense that we have been wronged in some way. We may feel disregarded, exploited or taken for granted. Anger is associated with a sense of injustice and our expectations of our partner's responsibilities. It can lead to a desire for revenge and reciprocity. The expression of anger leads to behaviours that see partners adjusting their conduct and reconciling to create a new understanding. If a new understanding is not created, it can lead to the end of the relationship.

Emotions can also stimulate group cohesion.[58] For example, at the end of a sporting event, fans of the winning team can experience strong joy, which can create a strong sense of cohesiveness among them. Similarly, if a person does something that evokes a sense of shame, they will adjust their behaviour to gain acceptance from their group. Alternatively, they may be so embarrassed that they want to flee the group and not return.

---

55 Goleman (1995).
56 Oatley, K., Keltner, D. and Jenkins, J.M. (2006). *Understanding Emotions*. Oxford: Blackwell.
57 Lutz, C. and White, G. (1986). 'The Anthropology of Emotions'. *Annual Review of Anthropology*, 15, 405–36.
58 Frijda, N.H. and Mesquita, B. (1994). 'The Social Roles and Functions of Emotions', in S. Kitayama and H. Marcus (eds), *Emotion and Culture: Empirical Studies of Mutual Influence*, Washington, DC: American Psychological Association, 51–87, p. 78.

Emotions also form an important part of our social interaction by the way they are expressed. We have already stated that the brain enables humans to use sophisticated vocal communication, but this is not our only form of emotional expression. The emotions we feel about our social relationships are also communicated through our body language. Our facial expressions, posture, vocal patterns and voice tones do a very efficient job of conveying our emotions. For example, a smile communicates positive emotion and indicates that we are open to social interaction.[59] A person who smiles a lot is perceived as happy, warm and attractive.

However, we are not always aware that we are expressing these emotions through our body, as this is often done subconsciously. You may successfully control what you say, but the tone of your voice and body language may say something totally different. This is called *emotional leakage*. This has important implications for you as a manager. For example, imagine you want a staff member to improve their performance and you are saying a number of complimentary things to inspire them. However, you then hear the same worker saying that you were angry and intimidated them. That may be because your body revealed your true frustrations with the worker. The existence of emotional leakage means that you must learn to monitor your body language and voice tones, even while in the middle of a conversation.

Sometimes our actions have little link to what caused the emotion. For example, in one study, people were made to hold their arms out horizontally for six minutes. It was found that those who did this were more critical of other people, even though those criticized had nothing to do with their predicament.[60] Another study had females immerse their arms in water that was either painfully cold or at room temperature. They were then given the option of rewarding or punishing another participant in the experiment. It was found that those who had their arms in the cold water were more likely to punish.[61] The pain of the water aroused negative emotions that were then released into the social environment.

This raises the issue of displaced emotions, or in this case *displaced aggression*. This is where anger is aroused by one thing, but then directed at someone

59 Deutsch, F.M, LeBaron, D. and Fryer, M.M. (1987). 'What is in a Smile?'. *Psychology of Women Quarterly*, 11(3), 341–52.
60 Berkowitz, L. (1990). 'On the Formation and Regulation of Anger and Aggression: A Cognitive-neoassociationistic Analysis'. *American Psychologist*, 45(4), 494–503.
61 Berkowitz, L., Cochran, S.T. and Embree, M.C. (1981). 'Physical Pain and the Goal of Aversively Stimulated Aggression'. *Journal of Personality and Social Psychology*, 40(4), 687–700.

or something that had nothing to do with the original cause. For example, a worker may have an argument with his wife, then come to work and be angry at his workmates. This has important implications for workplace management, particularly when trying to attribute the cause of a problem. The emotions you witness in the workplace may not have been caused by the victim of the anger. You may even find that you are angry with your staff for no obvious reason, because you are carrying emotions from a previous event.

As a manager, it is important to realize that you can also fall prey to displaced emotions. If something has raised your anger or anxieties, it may be wise to avoid doing anything important with a high social component. For example, if something has made you angry, it might be wise to defer any sensitive meetings until your emotions subside. The key is to recognize when your emotions are aroused in a way that can impact on your communication and performance.

A characteristic of emotions linked to displacement, is that *emotions can simmer*. Once the amygdala is activated, the chemicals that have been released can affect our mood for hours afterwards. They often simmer beneath our level of consciousness, so we may not be aware of them, but they certainly affect our mood, perception and behaviour. If we are upset by something early in the morning, we can still be carrying the emotion in the afternoon, and maybe even the evening. We may find that we snap at people for no reason or take offence where none is intended.

Once we are consciously aware of our emotions and our neo-cortex begins to evaluate the situation, we have a chance to act with a clearer head. For that reason, Daniel Goleman stresses the need for self-awareness. If we can recognize our emotions quickly and the impact they have on our lives, we can end destructive emotions quickly. Self-awareness requires a constant examination of our personal emotional and mental state, and with experience we become more adept at recognizing and managing our emotions.

However, sometimes we realize that we shouldn't be upset, but the emotion lingers and needs time to work its way out of our system. This can have implications when you have an upset staff member. Even when you have addressed their concerns, they may have a lingering anger which is no longer justified. In such cases, they merely need time to get it out of their system.

You need to get in the habit of identifying your individual moods and how they impact on your perceptions and awareness. If you gain the ability to identify changing emotional states, you can develop ways to work within your own limitations and those of others. You can develop your repertoire of responses so that, for example, if you are in the middle of a heated argument and you feel that you are about to explode, you can suddenly 'remember' that you have to make a call and ask if you can finish the conversation tomorrow. This gives you the chance to let your emotions subside, as well as giving you time to think about what they have been saying and develop a strategy to advance the issue.

Emotions can be a source of advantage in the workplace. For example, an activated limbic system can warn us that something is wrong and we need to take action, particularly when we have *gut feelings*. To understand gut feelings, consider the life of our ancestors, who would regularly encounter dangers in their natural world. They had to make decisions such as whether a berry is safe to eat or whether to walk down a track where a dangerous animal lived. Previous encounters with the berry or animal would have been recorded in the brain's emotional memory. When the danger was encountered again, the emotional memory was activated, sending us a gut feeling that something isn't right. We might not consciously remember the earlier interaction, but the aroused emotion would guide us to the safe option.

Memories are stored in different parts of the brain: for example, memories of sound are recorded in one part, while memories of smells are recorded in another. Memories of emotions are recorded in the amygdala. Every experience that generates an emotional response is recorded there, and is brought to our attention when we encounter a similar experience. This storehouse grows larger as we have more experiences in life, providing us with a sense of intuition. We build an emotional reservoir of wisdom and judgement which guides us through hunches or gut feelings.[62]

People's emotions fluctuate over time.[63] These fluctuations also occur in the workplace, and are often a result of what happens there.[64] As a manager, you can affect the work environment and the interactions that occur there, and this can help shape the nature of the emotions aroused at work. Your actions can influence the extent to which some negative or positive emotions are aroused, but not all.

---

62 Goleman (1998).
63 Watson, D. (2000). *Mood and Temperament*. New York: Guilford Press.
64 Ilies, R. Arvey, R.D. and Bouchard Jr, T.J. (2006). 'Darwinism, Behavioral Genetics, and Organizational Behavior: A Review and Agenda for Future Research'. *Journal of Organizational Behavior*, 27, 121–41.

Another factor affecting emotional variability is *temperament*. Researchers believe that temperament is determined by neuro-chemistry in the brain. As we've seen, emotions are located in the limbic system, in particular the part called the amygdala. However, people vary in the extent to which their amygdala is activated. Studies of children support the idea that temperament is biologically based. Studies have shown that some children have an amygdala that requires a lot of stimulation before it is aroused, so they can tolerate more aggravation before they get upset, while others children have a lower threshold.[65]

Differences in temperament can have implications for the workplace. A traffic controller's job may favour a cool-headed temperament, but an entertainer may require a temperament that easily expresses emotion. A workplace with low activated temperaments may become boring. On the other hand, a workplace full of hotheads is a manager's nightmare. No temperament type is better than another. For example, I once employed a tutor with a temperament which rarely ignited emotions. He was a dream to instruct, and never gave me any problems. However, I found that when I gave him case studies in which workers were getting upset, he had no idea what the problem was. He lacked empathy for those who were more readily aroused.

Since the publication of Goleman's book *Emotional Intelligence*, a large amount of research has been conducted on emotional intelligence in the workplace. The results show that managers with high emotional intelligence obtain better results from their employees.[66] Effective leaders manage their own feelings, recognize the emotions of their subordinates and intervene to enhance morale when necessary.[67] They develop an emotional radar to sense what others are feeling, and fine-tune their responses where appropriate.

While this chapter has identified many human limitations, it is important not to overstate them. For example, we might have an inflated sense of self-esteem, but not think we are perfect. We are highly rational, and cannot deny the years of learning that tell us otherwise. We know we goof. As humans, we have many failings, but our cognitive distortions do not negate the fact that

65 Kagan, J. (2005). 'Human Morality and Temperament', in G. Carlo and C.P. Edwards (eds), *Moral Motivation through the Lifespan*, Lincoln, NE: University of Nebraska Press, pp. 1–32.
66 Barbuto Jr, J.E. and Burbach, M.E. (2006). 'The Emotional Intelligence of Transformational Leaders: A Field of Elected Officers'. *Journal Social of Psychology*, 146(1), 51–64.
67 Cherniss, C. (2001). 'Emotional Intelligence and Organizational Effectiveness', in C. Cherniss and D. Goleman (eds), *The Emotionally Intelligent Workplace*, San Francisco, CA: Jossey-Bass, pp. 1–12.

we have significant mental ability. In the rest of this book, we will explore a number of workplace situations by drawing on these cognitive, motivational and emotional characteristics of humans.

3

Relationship Capital

The most important single ingredient in the formula of success is knowing how to get along with people.

US President Theodore Roosevelt

A 2005 study by Right Management Consultants found that about 35 per cent of managers who change jobs fail in their new ones. They either quit or are asked to leave within 18 months.[1] The main reason was a failure by managers 'to build strong relationships and team work with peers and subordinates', which accounted for 61 per cent of failures.

Researchers have long known about the importance of relationships in effective management. As early as 1956, a study by Robert Guest found that foremen working in the United States divided their time between their peers, their superiors and people inside their own work unit.[2] Two decades later, Henry Mintzberg confirmed the high level of interaction that characterized a manager's job. He noted that managers perform an important liaison role that requires making and maintaining contacts within and outside their organizations.[3]

Relationships are important for all levels of management. At upper levels, a 2011 study revealed that 'failure to build relationships and a team culture' was the most significant factor in corporate leadership failure. It scored 40 per cent, and was a dramatically more important cause of failure than 'poor communication' (11 per cent) or lack of vision (14 per cent).[4] At the other end of the corporate ladder, workers also state that relationships play an important role in their performance. In a 1996 study in New York, the two skills that workers considered most important were 'getting along with others at work' (chosen by 25 per cent) and 'establishing relationships built on trust' (22 per cent).[5]

1   Fisher, A. (2005). 'Starting a New Job? Don't Blow It'. *Fortune*, 7 March.
2   Guest, R.H. (1956). 'Of Time and the Foreman'. *Personnel*, May.
3   Mintzberg, H. (1973). *The Nature of Managerial Work*, New York: Harper & Row.
4   Sullivan, O. (2011). 'Global Leaders: Why They Succeed and Fail'. *Leadership Excellence*, 28, 8.
5   Frazee, V. (1996). 'Employees Value Workplace Relationships'. *Workforce Management*, 75(6), 25.

Relationships are important, as they are the mechanism through which we work. Organizations are built on people with skills and resources, and relationships are the links between those people. The efficiency of those links can have a significant impact on productivity, which is recognized in the phrase 'relationship capital'.

Relationship capital can be defined as the asset that is gained when managers develop and maintain relationships that help to achieve their work goals. Good relationships are an investment, and a valuable tool which we use to help attain our work goals. They pay significant dividends in times of stress and during peak times when we are under pressure to get things done.

In contrast, bad relationships are a liability. They can be emotionally draining and divert mental energy from work. Dealing with bad relationships can take up valuable time and lead to stress, which in turn undermines work performance. These factors can spill over into our home life, as emotions aroused at work are still simmering when we go home.

The concept of relationship capital is important as it recognizes that relationships have a tangible value that must be protected. Often, managers attend courses in interpersonal skills, but do not draw on those skills because of their anger. In a state of rage and with a sense of aggrievement, they forget the long-term implications of their actions. They do not act as if they are protecting an asset with economic value. Nor do they recognize the liabilities they create when they let their temper go. The concept of relationship capital recognizes this value and provides an incentive to manage relationships. It provides a motive to invest in functional relationships and apply the social skills managers may otherwise not be motivated to apply.

Referring to relationships as 'capital' may sound Machiavellian, in that human relationships are being managed for economic benefit. However, healthy relationships are also good for the individual. If a worker is in a good relationship, it can enhance the individual's sense of self-competence, identity and effectiveness in their professional role. Healthy relationships provide role models, a sense of acceptance and friendship,[6] which can help satisfy our core need for belonging.

---

6   Kram, K.E. (1988). *Mentoring at Work: Developmental Relationships in Organizational Life*, New York: University Press of America.

But how far do we take relationships? After all, friendships can become vehicles for indulgence,[7] and not everyone wants to be 'buddies' at work. Although you may become friends with your colleagues, that is not what we mean by the term 'relationship capital'. Relationship capital is not about becoming friends, but keeping relationship channels functional.[8] It is about maintaining relationships that help achieve work goals.

Relationship Management Strategies

One of the problems in creating relationship capital is the sheer diversity of relationships in the workplace. Not everyone wants the same thing from their colleagues. In 2003, Atkinson and Butcher conducted a study of management relationships and found that they fitted a number of patterns.[9] Some people do not want a close relationship at all, as one legal director noted of his colleague:

> *Andrew is a man of few words and totally task orientated. He is not interested in small talk or social niceties, so apart from jokes, which he likes, the conversation is focused around actual problems that need solutions .... He doesn't welcome personal relations with anybody in the office, and doesn't ever join in any of the social activities. It would be a thankless task to try and develop a relationship with him because he wouldn't welcome it.*[10]

In such instances, a good working relationship might exist, but it would be limited to work issues. Good working relationships can even exist when people do not like each other, as the following comment illustrates: 'Basically we just get on and do the job. There's no personal interaction at all. That's probably because we dislike each other .... But he's a good manager ... and he plays a straight game.'[11]

In this case, the relationship is strongly devoted to work issues, and even though they do not like each other, there is recognition that the other person has

7   Atkinson, S. (2004). 'Senior Management Relationships and Trust: An Exploratory Study'. *Journal of Management Psychology*, 19(6), 571–87.
8   Clydesdale, G. (2009). 'Management Education's Blind Spot: Management of Workplace Relations'. *Journal of European industrial Training*, 33(2), 178–91.
9   Atkinson, S. and Butcher, D. (2003). 'Trust in the Context of Management Relationships: An Empirical Study'. *SAM Advanced Management Journal*, Autumn, 24–35.
10 Ibid., p. 28.
11 Ibid.

integrity. This enables them to maintain a functional workplace relationship, but that is not always the case: 'Andrea only sees her own personal targets and will get there by driving hard come what may. She doesn't take anybody else into account along the way, so she's very difficult to work with.'[12]

In this case, Andrea is not trusted as a person and has trouble maintaining relationships. Trust is important in a relationship, but in some cases, a person might have integrity, but you still might not trust them to do what they say. Consider this statement from a worker in the hotel industry about a colleague:

> We are polite to each other, and that's really as far as it goes. By his own admission he has very little idea about how a hotel operates. I make no effort to see him because it would be a complete waste of my time. The poor man is not equipped. I just keep the relationship because politically I can't afford not to.[13]

In this case, the issue is not whether the person can be trusted to act with integrity. The issue is whether you can trust their ability to do the job. In this case, the manager has little faith in a colleague's ability, but recognizes that losing the relationship would be costly, so the strategy is to keep the relationship to a minimum. Finally, Atkinson and Butcher's research revealed that the workplace can create some very deep friendships: 'Our relationship is very personal. It's because of the way that the relationship has evolved. It just happens that we started working together here years ago.'[14]

These examples reveal the diversity of relationships that managers and workers must contend with. Some relationships are maximized by high levels of interaction, while others are best maintained by keeping interaction to a minimum to try to ensure that the relationship does not get worse. Some relationships are built purely around the job with little personal interaction, and they work well that way. In some cases, the colleague cannot be trusted, in which case, you have to reduce your vulnerability when dealing with that person.

An interesting aspect of the descriptions of workmates above is illustrated by the case of Andrea, who is seen as taking advantage of people. Her attitude has reached a point where others do not trust her and do not want to work with her. She has little relationship capital. This will have a significant

---

12 Ibid., p. 29.
13 Ibid., p. 28.
14 Ibid., p. 33.

impact on people's willingness to co-operate with her, and could affect her career prospects.

It is no surprise that many academics stress the importance of building trust in the workplace. However, Atkinson and Butcher's research shows a more sophisticated view of trust. There are different types of trust. There is trust in someone's integrity to do what they say, which Andrea lacks, but there is also trust in someone's ability. Many people have been let down by colleagues who have integrity but poor ability. It is not simply a case of building trust and being good. In fact, this research shows that in some instances, trust is not important for a relationship to function.

Another problem with placing too great an emphasis on building trust is that we run the risk of having a number of wide-eyed business graduates leaving themselves exposed to exploitation. You must minimize your exposure and avoid putting yourself in a position where you can be exploited. Nevertheless, you must expect disappointments, in which case the goal is not to eradicate losses, but to minimize them. The nature of conflicting goals, limited resources and human failings means you will always have disappointments.

In today's workforce, change occurs constantly. Workplace networks evolve and re-shape, and the person who can quickly establish useful work relationships has a significant productivity and competitive advantage. To illustrate this, David Rand, a psychologist at Harvard University, conducted an experiment in which participants played a simple game. Each player began with a certain number of points:

> As the game progresses, players have the opportunity to be either generous, and pay to give points to each player they are connected with, or be selfish, and do nothing. Following each round, some players are randomly given the opportunity to update their connections, based on whether other players have been generous or selfish.[15]

Rand found that players were likely to make and maintain connections with those who acted generously. They would break connections with those who behaved selfishly:

> 'People are more likely to form connections with people who are cooperative, and are much more likely to break those links with people

---

15   Reuell, P. (2011). 'Nice Guys Can Finish First'. *Harvard Gazette*, 14 November.

who are not,' Rand said. 'Basically, what it boils down to is that you'd better be a nice guy, or else you're going to get cut off.'[16]

Rand's research has important implications for the way you operate in the workplace. Relationships involve give and take. Those who do not give are not able to build relationships that help them achieve their goals. When we give, we are investing in relationship capital.

It is surprising that given the importance of workplace relationships, there has been very little academic research in this area. Psychologists have conducted significant research on romantic relationships, but much less on relationships at work. Nevertheless, some of the work on romantic relationships can be used to enlighten management.

The problem with applying concepts from romantic relationships to workplace relationships is their very different nature. These relationships have different characteristics in the exchange processes, including different levels of intimacy. Workplace relationships are based around work, but romantic relationships are based around the relationship. There is a far greater sense of emotion, commitment and sensitivity in romantic relationships. Nevertheless, we are still interested in these theories, as many of the components of relationships still exist, albeit with reduced intensity.

One concept from studies of intimate relationships that could be further explored in the workplace is *relationship maintenance strategies*.[17] These are behaviours that partners use to maintain a relationship after it has been established. They stop the relationship from deteriorating. The concept of maintenance strategies and behaviours has some relevance for management, and is an area where further research is needed.

Stafford and Canary (1991) identified strategies used to maintain a healthy relationship.[18] Three of particular relevance to the workplace include:

---

16 Ibid.
17 Baxter, L. and Dindia, K. (1990). 'Marital Partners' Perceptions of Marital Maintenance Strategies'. *Journal of Social and Personal Relationships*, 7, 187–208; Dindia, K. and Baxter, L. (1987). 'Strategies for Maintaining and Repairing Marital Relationships'. *Journal of Social and Personal Relationships*, 4, 143–58; Stafford, L. and Canary, D.J. (1991). 'Maintenance Strategies and Romantic Relationship Type, Gender and Relational Characteristics'. *Journal of Social and Personal Relationships*, 8, 217–42.
18 Stafford and Canary (1991).

1. **assurances** – in which one reassures the partner about their importance and the relationship;

2. **openness** – in which partners openly discuss feelings about the relationship;

3. **positivity** – where efforts are made to keep the interaction upbeat and enjoyable.

In 2000, Stafford, Dainton and Haas added two more behaviours:[19]

4. **advice** – expressions of opinions and support;

5. **conflict management** – which includes strategies such as co-operation and apologizing.

We could question the extent to which the first two strategies are relevant to the workplace, as many workers would find the idea of discussing emotions uncomfortable and superfluous to the job. On identifying emotional issues at work, it may be wiser for you, as a manager to limit yourself, and only discuss them if your colleague feels comfortable doing so. However, the third, fourth and fifth strategies have more relevance. Attempts should be made to keep interaction positive. The use of maintenance strategies and behaviours can contribute to a sense of equity and a healthier relationship.

Another element revealed in the literature on intimate relationships with relevance for the workplace is *relationship uncertainty*. This refers to 'the degree of confidence people have in their perceptions of involvement within close relationships'.[20] Many workers go through phases when they don't feel appreciated and may even wonder if a colleague likes them. One of our core motives is a 'sense of belonging', and there are times at work when this motive can feel unfulfilled. This can have implications for turnover and co-operative behaviour.

---

19 Stafford, L., Dainton, M. and Haas, S. (2000). 'Measuring Routine and Strategic Relational Maintenance: Scale Development, Sex versus Gender Roles, and the Prediction of Relational Characteristics'. *Communication Monographs*, 67, 306–23.
20 Knobloch, L.K. and Solomon, D.H. (1999). 'Measuring the Sources and Content of Relational Uncertainty'. *Communication Studies*, 50, 161–278, p. 264.

Relationship experts Knobloch and Solomon argue that reducing uncertainty is important for relationships.[21] They identified four types of uncertainty that can undermine a relationship:

1.   **uncertainty over behavioural norms** – what is considered to be acceptable and unacceptable behaviour in the relationship;

2.   **mutuality uncertainty** – uncertainty about the reciprocity of feelings between partners;

3.   **definitional uncertainty** – uncertainty about the current status of the relationship;

4.   **future uncertainty** – uncertainty about the long-range outcomes of the relationship.

This suggests that managers need to reduce uncertainty in their relationships. You may be totally unaware that someone at work is feeling unappreciated. Such feelings can fester and cause problems in the future, but can be nipped in the bud by simple friendly greetings. In the same way that work relationships have less intensity than romantic relationships, they often need less effort to maintain. They do not need long discussions about feelings. The correct tone of voice used in a greeting is a simple way of reducing uncertainty. Where there is uncertainty over behavioural norms, a manager or colleague can readily clarify these. Confirming expectations about what a worker can expect can help provide certainty and reduce anxieties.

Relationships are easier to manage when you know the person you are dealing with, but getting to know them takes time and requires a period of trial and error. By definition, this means you will make mistakes, in which case you need to show tolerance of your own mistakes and see them as a process of relational learning. Eventually, you will develop what Ricardi and Kurtz call 'mutually understood common ground'.[22] As you spend time and share experiences with your colleagues, you will find out more about their backgrounds, interests and beliefs, allowing you to establish the 'common

---

21 Knobloch, L.K. and Solomon, D.H. (2002). 'Information Seeking beyond Initial Interaction: Negotiating Relational Uncertainty within Close Relationships'. *Human Communication Research*, 28, 243–57.

22 Riccardi, V.M. and Kurtz, S.M. (1983). *Communication and Counselling in Health Care*, Springfield, IL: Charles C. Thomas.

ground that is needed in the development of trust and relationship'.[23] 'Knowing people means figuring people out – finding out what they hold true and dear and what their values are and their skills, weaknesses, and strengths.'[24]

Work relationships can change over time, and can develop in to friendships. Sias and Cahill studied peer friendships in the workplace, and noted that they can evolve from acquaintanceship to friendship, from friendship to close friendship, and from close friendship to almost best friendship.[25] Co-workers often become friends, and this is likely to occur when they work together in close proximity, share common ground and are involved in socializing outside the organization. In some cases, they can become best friends. Workmates often grow closer because of problems with their personal and/ or work life experiences. They are also more likely to grow closer the longer they spend together.

When workmates become friends, their communication becomes broader, more intimate and less cautious. Workers develop preferences to work with some people and not with others. Those preferences can be driven by similarity of values, interests or goals, and also by ethnic and demographic similarity.[26] In much the same way, those workers with whom communication is challenging, perhaps due to cultural or language proficiency differences, are also perceived to be poor candidates for early relationship investment.[27]

Preference for partners is also driven by the potential that person has to offer a reciprocal relationship. Those workers 'who offer few prospects of productive complementary exchanges get little attention, as do those failing to reciprocate in early exchange activity'.[28] For this reason, it is important that you do not demand too much from your colleagues. If you incur too many IOUs or are perceived as high-maintenance, people may choose not to reciprocate with you. New employees learn through experience whether the costs of a relationship match the benefits.

23 Slater, L. (2008). 'Pathways to Building Leadership Capacity'. *Educational Management Administration & Leadership*, 36(1), 55–69, p. 62.
24 Ibid.
25 Sias, P. and Cahill, D. (1998). 'From Co-workers to Friends: The Development of Peer Friendships in the Workplace. *Western Journal of Communication*, 62(3), 273–99.
26 Cole, T. and Teboul, J.C. (2004). 'Non-zero Sum Collaboration, Reciprocity and the Preference for Similarity: Developing an Adaptive Model of Close Relational Functioning'. *Personal Relationships*, 11, 135–60.
27 Ibarra, H. (1995). 'Race, Opportunity, and Diversity of Social Circles in Managerial Networks'. *Academy of Management Journal*, 38, 673–703.
28 Teboul, J.C. and Cole, T. (2005). 'Relationship Development and Workplace Integration: An Evolutionary Perspective'. *Communication Theory*, 15(4), 389–413.

Colleagues go through a process of relational learning. Their early interactions indicate whether a relationship is worth more investment. If early reciprocal and joint activities are profitable, it is likely to engender feelings of trust and create positive emotions that serve to encourage relational investment.[29] With a sense of trust and common understanding, their relationships become more complex and more valuable. Not only are they are more likely to co-operate with each other, but they are more likely to develop a feeling of being understood, which increases intimacy, satisfaction and loyalty.

Relationships may not stay like this for ever. Relational partners' interests, resources and goals can change over time.[30] This can affect the underlying sense of 'shared understandings', and partners may at times experience periods of relative ease and times of difficulty. For this reason, it may be necessary to re-evaluate relationships regularly.

Reciprocity is an important principle for guiding management interaction. It implies that if you want tolerance and support during your bad times, you should reciprocate. The challenge in establishing co-operation in organizations is getting it started. Consequently, managers should be pro-active, so that when your workmates consider future activities, they will act in reciprocity to the way you treated them in the past.[31] When you begin this cycle, you are actively investing in relationship capital. Consider the following experience of a manager in an educational institution:

> *Today I made my worst blunder since my appointment here. I was rushing to get a report written for the CEO. At the same time, I had to write an educational column for the local newspaper and I had to re-forecast the school's budget.*
>
> *I received a financial report from the financial centre showing that the school had over-spent on student supplies; I immediately sent this report off to the section managers for an urgent response. I hadn't thoroughly checked the report before sending it off, and unbeknown to me, it contained highly confidential salary scales for all staff, including the management team. Clearly, this was a case where I reached (or exceeded) my ability to process all of this information. I had exceeded my limited span of absolute judgement.*

29 Ibid.
30 Ibid.
31 Falk, A. and Gachter, S. (1999). 'Intrinsic Motivation and Extrinsic Incentives in a Repeated Game with Incomplete Contracts'. *Journal of Economic Psychology*, 20(3), 251–84.

As it turned out, the manager received only slightly negative comments. He noted: 'I think I have got off relatively lightly here. This could have been very serious. I have attributed this to the good relationship capital I have developed over time.' In this case, the staff did not approve of his actions, and the manager knew he had acted with haste. Relationship capital is not an excuse for shoddy behaviour. Staff would want to be assured that this would never happen again, but the matter did not create more work because of the capital he had invested in over time. The forgiveness he received was reciprocity for his previous actions.

Sadly, you may find that you put yourself out for people who do not reciprocate. Part of relationship learning involves discovering who is open to co-operative relationships, who is exploitive, and the limits to which some people are prepared to go. You may feel some people owe you, but never repay. It means that some of your work on developing relationships may seem wasted. Investments in relationships are similar to financial investments – some pay, some don't!

Psychologists have developed a number of theories that have reciprocity as their basis. Social Exchange Theory suggests that most relationships are based on some form of exchange.[32] The concept of social exchange seems applicable to the workplace, as most work is based on exchange – in particular, pay for work. However, exchange can go further than that, and include material, social or emotional exchange.

Another concept based on reciprocity with relevance to management is *psychological contracts*. Psychological contracts are a person's beliefs about what is expected of others in relationships.[33] The concept of contracts suggests that whenever people are involved in relationships, they have certain expectations about what things will be like in those relationships. These expectations guide what we expect of others in the same way as if we had a legal contract with them. Consequently, if those expectations are not met, there is a sense of violation of trust. Therefore, in order to ensure a functioning contract, a manager should act in the expected manner, for example meeting deadlines, delivering on promises, and spending time sharing personal values and goals.

---

32 Thibaut, J.W. and Kelly, H.H. (1959). *The Social Psychology of Groups*, New York: John Wiley and Sons.
33 Robinson, S.L. and Morrison, E.W. (2000). 'The Development of Psychological Breach Violation. A Longitudinal Study'. *Journal of Organizational Behavior*, 21(5), 525–46.

Hatfield, Utne and Traupmann (1979) believe that we look for equity in relationships. We look at what we put into a relationship and compare it to what our partners are putting in. We make judgements about the fairness of our contribution to relationships by comparing each partner's ratio of input to outcomes (relational comparison) and comparing our contributions to others in similar relationships (referential comparisons).[34] Such comparisons can provide a basis for managing relationships. If we are in an inequitable relationship, we can restore perceived equity by:

- changing our own contributions to the relationship;

- convincing our partner to change theirs;

- convincing ourselves that the inequity does not exist;

- ending the relationship.

Social exchange theory, psychological contracts and the reciprocity principle all reveal that expectations play an important role in relationships. For example, people have different expectations of what is considered reciprocal, and this can undermine relationships. Similarly, we may know how much we have done to help another person, but we are not always aware of how much they have done to help us. This uncertainty can place us in positions of unnecessary conflict.

Attribution theory can contribute to our understanding of expectations. Attribution theory refers to where we attribute the cause of an action. If we are harmed by a person, do we assume they did it on purpose, or do we accept that there were extenuating circumstances? William Ury, who co-founded Harvard University's programme on negotiation, states that when we deal with someone we know and like, we tend to attribute adverse events to extenuating circumstances: for example, 'I guess she didn't show up to the meeting because she was ill.'[35] However, if we are let down by someone we don't like, we tend to attribute bad outcomes to that person's basic nature. This suggests that if workers have a positive relationship with their colleagues, they will be more inclined to give them the benefit of the doubt, and this can reduce conflict.

---

34 Hatfield, E., Utne, M.K. and Traupmann, K. (1979). 'Equity Theory and Intimate Relationships', in R.L. Burgess and T.L. Huston (eds), *Social Exchange in Developing Relationships*, New York: Academic Press.
35 Ury, W. (1993). *Getting Past No: Negotiating in Difficult Situations*, New York: Bantam, p. 49.

For that reason, Ury suggests: 'The best time to lay the foundations for a good relationship is before a problem arrives.'[36] In other words, we should actively build relationship capital.

Sadly our attributions are not totally rational, and are one area where our cognitive capabilities can be distorted. Psychologists have shown that we can be prone to what they call the 'fundamental attribution error', a tendency we humans have when making attributions about other people to underestimate the influence of external factors and overestimate the influence of internal or personal examples. Ironically, when we attribute our own actions, we do the opposite – a tendency psychologists call 'self-serving bias', in which we have a tendency to attribute our own success to internal factors such as ability or effort, while putting the blame for failure on external factors such as fate or luck.

Another factor from our model of human nature that has relevance to relationships is Social Comparison Theory, which states that individuals compare their position to those around them, and this tendency can be very destructive on our relationships. First, we tend to make comparisons with those who are closest to us – our most immediate form of comparison – and this can give rise to jealousy, or what has been called 'frenvy' (envy of friends). It can also mean that in order to preserve our own self-esteem, we can make negative comparisons with others. We also have to be aware how our achievements may affect others. If you celebrate and make a noise about your success, a workmate going through social comparison may feel disappointed with their own achievement. They may feel that you are showing off or indirectly putting them down.

The importance of social comparison for managers can be seen when you come to praise your staff. Recognizing the achievements of a good staff member may have detrimental effects. It may make the other workers feel bad. This does not mean you should not recognize achievement, but you need to be sensitive to the positive and negative effects. This means doing it in such a way that others feel that they can emulate this success. Recognition can motivate others, or deflate them.

However, most people are not too mean-spirited when they see others being rewarded. People believe that someone who works harder deserves greater reward, as suggested by Adams' Equity Theory, which was developed

---

36 Ibid., pp. 49–50.

to address fairness in employee–employer relationships.[37] According to the theory, a person perceives and assesses their own inputs to a relationship in comparison with their partner's inputs and outputs. Workers will look at what they contribute to a job, and what they get out of it. They will then compare this to other workers. If others are getting more or contributing less, the worker will lose motivation. In this theory, the work relationship is still based on exchange, but in comparing themselves to others, they are also considering fairness or equity.

The basis of these theories is exchange and fairness. They do not suggest we treat everyone the same, because some people contribute more than others. These theories argue that we should contribute to relationships in a reciprocal manner. You should make a contribution or investment into a relationship in proportion to the investment that your colleague makes.

Why Do We Destroy Relationship Capital?

Sadly, we can destroy relationship capital with very little effort, and there are a number of reasons for this. First, we may feel we have been mistreated and 'they shouldn't be able to get away with it'. We seek justice and reciprocity. Seen in this light, we may feel justified in abusing our colleagues.

Sometimes we undermine relationships without even knowing it. For example, it may be that you have just finished house renovations that have turned out wonderfully, so you tell your workmates how you have finally created your dream home. You tell them, 'It's the best house in the area and much better than those cheap looking houses on the south side.'

On the face of it, there is nothing wrong with what you have said. It may be perfectly true, and you have every right to be happy. But imagine that one of your workmates lives in one of those cheap-looking houses on the south side. Clearly, you didn't say it to offend them, and because of that, you didn't realize that you had offended them. However, your unwitting insult can spark off a descending spiral of reciprocity. You may find they lower their opinion of you and co-operate less. It is possible that your workmate may accept that your house is nicer, but cognitive dissonance kicks in, and they may begin

---

37 Adams, J.S. (1965). 'Inequity in Social Exchange', in L. Berkowitz (ed.), *Advances in Experimental Psychology*, vol. 2, New York: Academic Press, pp. 267–99.

to identify faults in your work that make them feel better about themself. Of course, in your eyes, they are starting the negativity.

It is so easy to offend people without knowing it. It happens because we are not always aware of the implications of what we say. Our limited spans of judgement make it particularly easy to do so, particularly when we are focusing on other issues, and it is not always worth the time and mental energy to think through all the possible implications of what we say. Nor can we be aware of every sensitivity that a workmate carries with them. Unfortunately, we may believe we have not offended anyone when the reality is very different. We hope that workmates do not attribute any misunderstanding to a desire to put them down, but even if they interpret our motives correctly, we may still present an image of insensitivity or arrogance.

A second way you may destroy relationship capital is because you are frustrated with someone because their behaviour does not meet your expectations. Once again, this can be linked to reciprocity and exchange theories of relationships. We may feel that we are contributing a lot to a relationship, but not getting an equal return. These feelings are consistent with the frustration-aggression hypothesis developed by psychologists. It is natural to become frustrated when our expectations are not met, and frustration gives birth to feelings of aggression.

Solutions have been suggested by the Roman philosopher Seneca, who believed that we set our expectations too high when dealing with other people. He suggested that we should lower our expectations and accept that people might not see things the same way we do. Seneca's suggestion may be wise. We can have expectations of others that are artificially high. We can also have self-serving bias when assessing our own contributions. However, in some cases, your workmates may indeed not be pulling their weight, and you need to talk it through with them. You may discover that they have been doing more work behind the scenes than you were not previously aware of. Alternatively, they may have been slacking and taking advantage of you, in which case the goal is to talk to them about the issue without being offensive or emotional.

Emotions can also undermine our relationships, the most obvious example being what Goleman called *limbic hijack*,[38] where something upsets us and the limbic structure takes over our brain's activities. We become driven by emotions, not rational thought, and the affect on our relationships can be disastrous. As

---

38 Goleman, D. (1995). *Emotional Intelligence*, New York: Bantam Books.

a manager, it is important that you learn to recognize when your emotions are changing, and act to limit their effect. This may mean withdrawing from conversations when you feel your emotions are destructive. As a manager, you also need to identify when your colleagues and staff are becoming agitated. However, you must be careful how you handle this. Telling someone that they are getting aggressive or losing control can be taken as an insult, and can undermine healthy relationships. It may also be that their emotions are legitimate given the way they feel they have been treated.

Another characteristic of emotions that can undermine relationships is the fact that emotions can simmer, so we may carry them from one situation in to another. In some cases, it may lead us to be oversensitive, or it may lead us to be aggressive in situations that do not warrant it. Sometimes positive emotions can also be displaced, like the manager who on hearing good news walks into a sensitive meeting cracking jokes and flirting with the female staff. This can also undermine relationships.

Even when controlling your emotions, unexpressed feelings can be 'leaked' through your body language and tone of voice, and if picked up by your colleagues, may result in an aggressive response. It is also important not to place too much weight on aggressive things said in the heat of discussion. Even good people can be overcome by their limbic structure and act as if they are an animal under attack. Good people can have bad emotions.[39]

Relationships may also be undermined by the fact that people have different schemas about the world and the way it works. If people hold different views, it is only natural that some level of conflict may occur. This is not necessarily a bad thing, as the resulting discussion can provide two different views of confronting an issue. In such circumstances, the key is to keep focused on the issue and avoid becoming emotional or personal in your comments. However, in heated discussions, emotions do get aroused, and if allowed to escalate, can easily erode relationship capital.

It is important to acknowledge that your views are built on a lifetime of learning, but so too are your colleagues'. It is natural that your views will seem more cognizant given your personal learning process, but it would be ignorant to believe that yours is the only learning path. They key in all cases is to avoid emotional arousal or insulting their experience or esteem.

---

39 Stone, D., Patton, B. and Heen, S. (1999). *Difficult Conversations: How to Discuss What Matters Most*, London: Michael Joseph.

Dealing with Difficult People

In many workplace settings, you will have to deal with people with whom it is hard to develop relationships. Some people are just plain 'difficult', with poor social skills that make them hard to get along with. However, research on difficult people suggests that in many cases, something else may be going on. Duff and Hollingshead claim that we call someone 'difficult' or 'bad' because they obstruct and create difficulties in our work.[40] This would suggest that someone who does not respond to our normal way of working would be considered difficult, but the problem may not be their personality: it may be the limitations of our own working mode.

Finlay (2005) studied 'difficult' nurse–patient relationships, and found that at times the difficulty did not reflect the individuals involved, but the work processes at the time.[41] This is supported by another study which found that whether nurses labelled patients 'good' or 'bad' depended on what was going on in the ward.[42] The availability of supplies and equipment and whom they were working with all affected whether a nurse was likely to label a patient as 'difficult'. A key issue was how much time was available. If nurses had time to get to know their patients, there were few problems; however, with less time, difficulties arose. When nurses were pressed for time, they would enforce rules such as visiting hours and rush patients through care, limiting their choices.[43] On such occasions, patients were more likely to be perceived as 'difficult'. These studies revealed how work context can affect relationships, and context is something that you can control as a manager.

Over years at work, we develop ways of doing things and expect people to fit in when we do our job, but if someone does not fit in, we view them as uncooperative or just plain difficult. It is understandable that you might want to change your work techniques, but the problem may be that you lack flexibility. Consider the following example, described by a Quality Control Officer from a general hospital:

> *The Quality Control Officer received feedback from one of their patients who was about to have an operation. The patient had visited the*

---

40 Duff, R. and Hollingshead, A. (1968). *Sickness and Society*, New York: Harper & Row.
41 Finlay, L. (2005). 'Difficult Encounters'. *Nursing Management*, 12(1), 31–6.
42 Johnson, M. and Webb, C. (1995). 'Rediscovering Unpopular Patients: The Concept of Social Judgement'. *Journal of Advanced Nursing*, 21, 466–75.
43 MacDonald, M. (2007). 'Origins of Difficulty in the Nurse–patient Encounter'. *Nursing Ethics*, 14(4), 510–21.

hospital's website and found little information on what he could expect when he is in hospital, e.g.: does his room have a TV, can he bring a laptop, what times meals are served, etc.

The Quality Control Officer asked the charge nurse to ring the patient and answer his queries. However, the Charge Nurse responded by saying she would not phone him as it was a waste of time and she had already sent him information about his operation.

To prevent a small issue from escalating, the Quality Control Officer phoned the patient and provided him with the information he was seeking. She discovered that although the patient was asking about the routine, the real issue was about his anxiety levels and not knowing what to expect. She answered his questions and helped reduce his nervousness about the operation.

The Quality Control Officer then told the Charge Nurse that she had made the call. The nurse responded by saying that she did actually phone the patient, but it was a waste of time as 'he didn't ask one question about his operation or surgery, and he was only in for one night, and that his surgery was minor anyway'. In her eyes, the patient was unnecessarily demanding. As a health professional, she focused on the surgery, which was minor. But it was a wider issue. She had missed the point that he was going to be in an unknown environment and outside his comfort zone.

A study of nurses by Pam Smith suggests that putting people in the 'difficult' category can allow workers to distance themselves emotionally from them and cope better with their workload.[44] In this case, there may be short-term advantages in categorizing someone as 'difficult'. However, this assessment does not reflect the processes involved, and can be a big problem if we have an ongoing work relationship with them.

It may be that the difficult person is making demands of you that you feel are unnecessary or you are uncomfortable with. When dealing with such people, Finlay suggests that we should first evaluate why we have evaluated someone as 'difficult'.[45] Are we trying to express our own uncertainty, or are we alerting others to the complexities of the problems involved? Are we deflecting a challenging

---

44 Smith, P. (1992). *The Emotional Labour of Nursing*, London: Macmillan.
45 Finlay (2005).

situation into the 'difficult' category, perhaps because it is taking up more time than we can commit? Finally, if we designate someone as 'difficult', what does it tell us about ourselves and our relationship with the 'difficult' person?

Not all difficult situations are a consequence of the context. Sometimes the people we are dealing with are being unfair. Consider the example below of a manager of a conservation team:

> *I spent the first of three days in the field with a team to re-measure a wetland vegetation monitoring plot. My role was to obtain the previous datasets and to accompany the field team. There was a problem due to the length of time between monitoring occasions and that another employee had taken and not returned the original data. Due to time constraints and priorities, I did not adequately source enough information (a clear failing on my part).*
>
> *I held a staff meeting and apologized to the team for not getting all the data. Warren, the technical support officer was exasperated with the failing of monitoring data, and voiced his concerns. He repeated a number of times that this was a problem. He was clearly in an emotional state. I let all the staff express themselves, but Warren continued to go on about it. Ideas were discussed to address the issue but he claimed all options were wrong.*
>
> *I certainly thought about telling Warren not to go on about it. I felt my authority and skills were being overly criticized. I almost told him to 'pull his head in'.*

This situation is interesting, in that again the boss made a mistake and acknowledged it, but this left him exposed to attack from one of his staff. This book stresses the need to protect the self-esteem of your staff. This also applies to managers. You are not there to be exposed to continuous ridicule. Argyle and Henderson (1985) suggested that rules should be taught for conducting and maintaining relationships.[46] These would include 'accept one's fair share of workload' and 'don't criticize co-workers publicly'.

The rules suggested by Argyle and Henderson are valuable, in that they reflect what would be considered common sense, but there are situational factors to be considered in the application of any rules, and some of their rules

---

46 Argyle, M. and Henderson, M. (1985). *The Anatomy of Relationships*, London: Heinemann.

embody an ethical framework which might not be shared. Sometimes it is best to keep it simple. A road-laying company had one spoken rule: 'Play the ball not the man.' This sporting analogy was fully understood by the predominantly male staff. It meant that if there was a problem, you discussed the issue, not the worker. If such a rule pervades the culture, it can help keep peace in the workforce and focus staff on work, not personalities.

One of the best books to explore difficult situations was written by Stone, Patton and Heen. Entitled *Difficult Conversations*, it reveals how emotions, esteem and identity can affect difficult communication.[47] The authors actually go as far as to say that difficult conversations embody three ulterior conversations shaped by these characteristics of human nature. We have a tendency to think of exchanges as 'what happened' conversations, in which we discuss the issue at hand, however emotions are so important that they actually constitute a second conversation: the 'feelings' conversation. The third conversation is the 'identity' conversation, which reveals what this conversation says about us.

We might think that the 'what happened' conversation should be straightforward, as you merely need to reassess the facts of the issue. However Stone, Patton and Heen state that 'difficult conversations are almost never about getting the facts right. They are about conflicting perceptions, interpretations and values'.[48] The task for you as a manager is not to explore who is right and who is wrong, but to explore each other's interpretation, as each party will have different information.

The emotional conversation involves recognizing how your opponent's feelings may be affected by the discussion, and also how your own emotions are affected. Are your own emotions valid given what has happened, or are you over-reacting? Stone Patton and Heen state that 'difficult conversations do not just involve feelings, they are at their very core about feelings'.[49] In fact, sometimes feelings are all that matters. Consider the hospital example above, in which the Charge Nurse perceived a patient as 'difficult'. She only considered the 'what happened' conversation, whereas the real issue was emotional, in particular the patient's anxieties about the operation.

---

47   Stone, Patton and Heen (1999).
48   Ibid., p. 10.
49   Ibid., p. 13.

The identity conversation refers to what this means to the two people involved in terms of their sense of who they are in the world, and what it says about their esteem and identity: for example, in the scenario described above where you criticized the cheap housing on the south side and unintentionally offended the self-esteem of your colleague, and maybe their identity if they feel a strong sense of identification with their house. To further understand these differences, consider this situation:

> *On a hot summer's day, a manager walks past one of his production teams and notices that two of her staff are arguing. She asks 'What's the problem?'*
>
> *Reuben answers 'I've been sitting here all day with the window open, enjoying the breeze. It's hot. Then 15 minutes ago, Paul comes in as if he owns the place and shuts the window because a truck comes along and makes a noise.'*
>
> *The manager can hear the truck. It is still there, and very loud. Paul defends himself: 'Why are you going on about this? I've given in to you. I've opened the window even though that noise is loud and affecting my work.'*
>
> *Reuben answers back: 'The truck will be gone soon – it only started when you arrived.' The truck is very loud, and you realize that 15 minutes of this could affect their work.*
>
> *'Stop the moaning. I gave in to you,' says Paul. The window is open as Reuben requested, and Paul is still having to put up with the noise, but Reuben is the one complaining. He has a reputation for being moody.*

If we look at the facts, Reuben seems to have gone too far. Paul had a genuine concern with the noise levels, but nevertheless gave in to Reuben and had opened the window some time ago. On the face of it, Reuben is wrong to still be moaning. However, if we focus on identities, we discern a very different conversation. The conversation is now about Paul coming in as if he owns the place and shutting the window without considering Reuben. The conversation is no longer about an open or closed window – it is about Paul's lack of respect for Reuben. Seen in this light, Paul is in the wrong.

However, if we look at it as an emotional conversation, we get arrive at another interpretation. Initially, we may see Paul as being wrong in upsetting a fellow staff member, and it may be that he did it deliberately, as he knows Reuben is moody and perhaps he knew he wanted the window open. On the other hand, Reuben is moody. His emotions are legitimate, but they may be disproportionate to the event.

Dissecting this conversation into facts, emotions and identity leads to three different assessments, and you, as a manager, need to address all issues if you are to solve this problem effectively. Emotions and identity issues are just as important as the issue at hand if you want to maintain good staff relations.

Stone, Patton and Heen's technique offers an effective way to deal with difficult conversations and maintain productive relationships. They do this by including human characteristics, whose importance is too often overlooked. Work issues such as pay rises or work reorganization can be dealt with more efficiently when we consider how rejections or changes impact on colleagues' emotions and sense of identity. Manoeuvring through sensitive interactions involves addressing all three conversations.

But what do you do when dealing with someone who doesn't want to co-operate? William Ury addressed this question in his book *Getting Past No*.[50] At times you will deal with people bent on attack and counter-attack, driven by anger, suspicion and interests that appear irreconcilable. Ury's approach was to change the discussion from attacking each other to attacking the problem, but this can be hard to do when your colleague is full of historical baggage, a sense of aggrievement and highly charged emotions.

Ury suggested that we follow five steps in order to address such situations. His approach recognizes the very human elements we described in our model. Ury acknowledges that you will want to fight back and you will be full of emotion, hence his first step is 'don't react', or what he calls 'go to the balcony'. This is the same as taking time out to regain your composure. You take yourself to a psychological balcony, where you can step back and collect your thoughts. It means distancing yourself from your natural desire to fight back. You leave, and you do not re-engage until your neo-cortex is in control.

In the second step, Ury suggests you step to their side. Let them talk, and you need to listen actively. This does not mean that they are allowed to be verbally offensive, and you may need to ask questions that redirect them to the issue at hand. Your questions will show them that you are listening. As you

---

50 Ury (1993).

begin to understand their view, you should acknowledge it and their feelings. By doing so, you can help diffuse their anger. Ury recognizes the importance of self-esteem and emotion. You must acknowledge your colleague's abilities and qualities as a person, and in some cases you may need to apologize for any offence or pain felt.

Apologizing for offence is not the same as admitting you were wrong. There was probably a reason why you took the stand you did. Your emotions and position are equally valid. This puts you in a situation where you need to acknowledge their view while not weakening your own position. You may need to explain why you hold your view. However, if your view is the polar opposite to your colleague's, this could reignite a sequence of defence and attack. Hence, Ury's third stage is to re-frame the discussion. You need to 'change the game', from defining positions to solving problems. Ask your opponent why they hold their position, to discover what truly motivates them. Every time they speak, they are giving you information you may be able to use to solve the problem. The goal is to find other ways to solve the problem.

Sadly, some people will still refuse to co-operate and will continue to attack you, in which case they may need to be reminded how the negotiation should be conducted. You need to identify what it is that is stopping them from agreeing. For example, it may be they are scared of losing face if they are seen to give in to you, so you need to arrive at a solution that protects their self-esteem. Ury calls this building a 'golden bridge' that allows them to overcome their barriers. This may not mean satisfying their unmet interests, but it definitely involves protecting their self-esteem.

Finally, Ury says that you must be very careful how you use your power. In difficult conversations, it is very tempting to cut to the chase and remind your opponent of your managerial authority. In some cases, it may be necessary to remind them of what will happen if they don't come to an agreement, but this may be detrimental in the long term.

The way you treat conflict lays the foundations for your future interactions. If your colleague feels that they have given in to you, they will expect reciprocity in the future. To establish a lasting relationship, you need to address their concerns and give them an element of choice. The overall goal is to turn your adversary in to a partner with a joint concern for developing the best solution. To do this, you must turn such conflicts in to problem-solving meetings.

This raises the question of forgiveness. What role does forgiveness play in the workplace? Forgiveness is one way in which individuals can repair damaged relationships and overcome debilitating thoughts and emotions.[51] A number of forgiveness strategies exist, including making an effort to understand the offender's motives, engaging in constructive dialogue, giving time or attention to the offender, or acknowledging one's own role in causing or contributing to the offence. As attribution theory suggests, it may be wise to examine the role of the environment when the event took place. Such strategies do not mean forgetting the offence. Forgetting would leave you exposed to a repeat performance. Forgiveness strategies involve altering how one thinks, feels and behaves towards the offender, even when it may be within one's moral right to pursue retribution and experience anger and resentment.[52]

When people forgive, they willingly sacrifice some of their interests for the sake of their partner or the relationship,[53] but forgiveness would seem to make sense given the long-term nature of workplace relationships. Whereas one can usually walk away from unpleasant interactions in a social setting, it is often very difficult to sever negative relationships in the workplace because of the continued need to interact as part of your job.

The problem with forgiveness is that it may not address an underlying sense of injustice. We previously discussed how the reciprocity principle means that we feel comfortable repaying goodness. However, it can also mean that we want to repay people for perceived harm. This can lead to an ongoing cycle of ill will. To avoid this escalation of harm and the resulting costs, it may be necessary to cut your losses, but it can be hard to let go.

This negative aspect of reciprocity has plagued some of the world's greatest thinkers. It is referred to in the Bible. Jesus, concerned with the Old Testament's interpretation of reciprocity, said:

> *You have heard that it was said, 'an eye for eye, and a tooth for tooth'. But now I tell you, do not take revenge on someone who wrongs you. If anyone slaps you on the right cheek, let them slap your left cheek too ....*[54]

51 Aquino, K., Grover, S.L., Goldman, B. and Folger, R. (2003). 'When Push Doesn't Come to Shove: Interpersonal Forgiveness in Workplace Relationships'. *Journal of Management Inquiry*, 12(3), 209–16.
52 Ibid.
53 Van Lange, P.A.M., Rusbult, C.E., Drigotas, S.M., Arriaga, X.B., Witcher, B.S. and Cox, C.L. (1997). 'Willingness to Sacrifice in Close Relationships'. *Journal of Personality and Social Psychology*, 72, 1,373–95.
54 Luke 6:29–30.

However, one of the difficulties with the claim that forgiveness is beneficial in relationships is that people may take advantage of it. Not surprisingly, Aquino et al. have come to the conclusion that 'it is unlikely that forgiveness improves relationships under all circumstances'.[55] When considering your response, it is important to consider the likely length of your future relationship with that person and the extent to which any reprisal could escalate and affect future action. If you are likely to be working with that person for some time, your reprisal may not resolve the issue, but may create a bigger long-term problem.

Teboul and Cole studied the use of forgiveness, and found that people balance the benefits of a relationship against the costs. They state: 'When infractions are detected, individuals are inclined to forgive as long as the benefit accrued from exchange and coordination outweighs the cost of continued investment in such a relationship.'[56] If the costs outweigh the benefits, individuals become aware of the unfavourable relationship development. There may be relational uncertainty, in which case the worker may seek information to determine the discrepancy between expectation and reality.[57] This may involve talking to other colleagues about the problem. The outcome of such investigations can lead individuals to either change their own behaviour, try to change their partners' transgressions, or pursue relational opportunities elsewhere.[58]

An alternative approach is *tolerance*, which is described as 'the ability to accept something while disapproving of it'. It can mean that you have to support a practice, action or decision of your colleagues even though you disagree with it.[59] Your workmates and work context will never be completely to your liking, so tolerance is a strategy you will have to resort to at times. This can be difficult, and you will experience times when you rationally accept the need for tolerance but your emotions are still simmering. You may need to combine tolerance with avoidance strategies to avoid blowing it.

Relationships are a key characteristic of the human species. They are what enable us to create the organizations that you will eventually manage. This chapter recognizes that relationship capital is an investment that can help you to achieve your performance objectives. However, there are always issues to

55 Aquino et al. (2003), 214.
56 Teboul and Cole (2005).
57 Planalp, S. and Honeycutt, J.M. (1985). 'Events that Increase Uncertainty in Personal Relationships'. *Human Communication Research*, 11, 593–604.
58 Cole and Teboul (2004).
59 Prilipko, E.V., Antelo, A. and Henderson, R.L. (2011). 'Rainbow of Followers' Attributes in a Leadership Process'. *International Journal of Management and Information Systems*, 15(2), 79–94.

confront, limitations of compatibility and human failings that mean we need to develop relationship management strategies to protect what may be our most important workplace asset.

4

Constructive Management

He who lives without folly isn't as wise as he thinks.
François de la Rochefoucauld[1]

Some time ago, I rented out my house and engaged a rental agency to manage the contract with the tenant. The agent's job was to ensure that rents were paid and the house was kept in good condition. However when the tenant left, I discovered the house was a mess – lampshades were missing, there were holes in the walls, woodwork had been scratched, and a bathroom cabinet was found in the garden. When I pointed this out to Brenda, the agent, she was clearly shocked by how many things she had missed, and after she left the house, I noticed she was sitting in her car, crying.

I wrote to the agent's boss, suggesting their company introduce procedures to ensure this never happened again. First, I suggested that the photos they took when the tenant moved in should be used to compare the property's state when the tenant leaves. In my case, the agent had relied purely on her memory. Second, I suggested they use a physical checklist, and tick off the items as they went through the house. Third, I suggested that they give better training to staff on how to conduct an inspection. The agent's boss responded:

> *It is unfortunate that you had a bad experience with Brenda. I have been involved in Property Management for over 20 years and I can assure you that if anyone knows how to do this properly, it would be me. But I am unable to do everyone's inspections. I have been carrying out detailed checks on properties, taking numerous photos and attending to maintenance in a prompt fashion, long before most people thought it was necessary. Your recommendations are what I do routinely (and more).*

---

1   De la Rochefoucauld, F. (1871). *Reflections; Or Sentences and Moral Maxims by Francois Duc De La Rochefoucauld, Prince de Marsillac,* transl. J.W. Willis Bund and J. Hain Friswell, London: Simpson Low, Son, and Marston.

However, I can appreciate that your experience would make you feel the way you do. You are of course entitled to your opinion.

What is significant about the response is that the manager told me what she did when carrying out inspections. She did not say what she did to ensure that her staff did those things. Clearly, there were insufficient management structures in place for training and supporting staff. Consequently, staff were being set up for failure. Brenda, my agent, quit her job not long after. Not being an expert on management systems, she took the blame personally. It affected her self-esteem and happiness. She believed that she was not very good at this job.

It is interesting to wonder how many people leave their jobs because of poor performance. However, the cause of the problem may not be their lack of ability, but insufficient training and management. In theory, this should not happen in today's business world. Human resource (HR) specialists have developed a huge body of literature on performance appraisals and need assessments which should reveal skill deficiencies. These can then be signalled to staff training specialists, who can draw upon a number of training options.

However, there are a number of problems with formal staff training systems. First, not all companies are large enough to employ specialist HR and staff training divisions. Second, to justify the expense of staff training, a number of staff may need to have the same skill deficiency. Finally, some skills are tacit and are hard to address in any book or formal class. They are best taught on the job, by a supervisor who can draw on their own experience.

To give an example, consider the response of another property manager, Daryl. The following describes an occasion when he discovered that his employee John was making a serious omission:

*Where you have receipt of rent, you will probably have rental arrears. It is important to be on top of arrears as they can quickly balloon out ....
A case today was a new tenant who had paid the initial week only as part of the entry cost and was now two weeks in arrears. I rang her, and she said, 'But I am going to pay fortnightly.' I explained she needed to pay in advance. It took me some time to get the concept through to her as she was convinced John had told her differently.*

Who had failed here? Not her – us. We had failed to tell her what date to set up her automatic payment from … it may seem obvious but it wasn't to her.

The next day, I asked John about the form we give new tenants, which is a standard accounts payable form with our bank account details thereon, which has a provision for the commencement date. I asked him if he was filling in the date, and he said he wasn't. I asked how long he hadn't been doing this. He claimed he had never done it.

Now it was obvious that it was my fault for never checking his practices. The situation has been corrected now. I actually ended up sitting with John and getting him to go through all the steps of the letting process and to try and think of it as if he had just entered the working world.

I think by doing this, rather than assuming he knows these things and moreover, knows to convey these things, I create an environment whereby he considers all this and learns the skills himself.

These two examples of property managers show very different approaches to worker mistakes. In the first case, the worker took the blame and left the job with lower morale and confidence. In the second case, the manager took the blame and saw it as a chance not just to address the deficiency, but to ensure that all client directives were passed on. This helped his staff gain the knowledge necessary to achieve the standard desired.

On-the-job training is the most individualized of all training options as it deals directly with the needs of individuals as their problems arise. You do not have to wait until enough workers have the same problem to create a class and justify formal staff training. It is also a quicker way to upgrade skills. Documenting deficiencies and sending them to the HR department can take time, while managers are often in a position to address these instantly. On-the-job training is also cheaper as it avoids the cost of arranging and paying for staff training specialists. Finally, the training can help to develop the relationship between workers and managers. Managers gain respect for their knowledge while helping the workers to grow.

Kennedy, Lawton and Plumlee (2002) state that before educators teach a particular ability, they first need to teach their students that they do not know something.[2] It is highly tempting for a boss to bring their workers to their senses by blatantly pointing out their faults and criticizing their work, and many managers adopt such an approach. A recent study found that 38 per cent used leadership behaviours such as always pointing out mistakes and encouraging staff to criticize others.[3] However, such an approach can be very destructive and may create barriers to learning and commitment.

Many old-time coaches used to give their charges a good kick up the backside to motivate them. However, this can be counterproductive. Recalling our model of human nature, such criticism can have a huge impact on a worker's self-identity and self-esteem, which in turn can reduce their sense of belonging with the organization. Harsh criticism can create a sense in the worker that 'I don't belong here.'

Cognitive dissonance may be aroused when workers hear criticism, even when that criticism is justified. It may create a gap between how the workers want to perceive themselves (their ideal selves) and reality (their real selves). In some cases, this can motivate the workers to improve. However, it can also lead to a number of other responses. Other common reactions to cognitive dissonance include 'denial', in which the worker does not accept the criticism, creating a huge barrier to learning. A second common response is the worker may downplay the importance of the area where they are weak, which can reduce their motivation to learn the task. Finally, they may prefer to focus on areas where they are strong, and come to the conclusion that they are in the wrong job.

These examples show how destructive inappropriate training can be, yet by definition some criticism must be warranted, otherwise they would not need the training. This highlights the importance of how training is carried out. Criticism is more likely to be accepted if accompanied by praise or comments that sustain self-esteem. For example, you could maintain their self-esteem by recognizing their potential, then show them how to achieve that potential. It is often wise to give a compliment that makes the following criticism easier to bear.

Learning processes must protect the self-esteem of the worker, and not let criticism and their disappointment undermine their motivation, identification and commitment to the job. This can be achieved by continually reminding them

---

2   Kennedy, E.J., Lawton, L. and Plumlee, E.L. (2002). 'Blissful Ignorance: The Problem of Unrecognized Incompetence and Academic Performance'. *Journal of Marketing Education*, 24(3), 243–52.
3   McCarthy, S. (2009). *The Leadership Culture Performance Connection: Transforming Leadership and Culture – The State of the Nations*. Plymouth, MI: Human Synergistics.

of their ability to overcome these weaknesses, and your faith in their potential. You can also remind them of other areas where they have performed well.

A problem with staff training is that workers often don't know what they don't know, and the least competent workers are often the most ignorant. This is known as the Dunning-Kruger effect, which refers to the fact that people who don't know how poorly they perform also lack the skills to judge what actually constitutes good performance. Individuals can only judge their competence if they are sufficiently competent to do so.[4] The skills required to judge ability are the same ones required to do well in that job. Not only is this a problem for staff training, it can be a nightmare when handling performance evaluations and promotional rounds. Your life could be made much easier if your staff had the full ability to recognize good performance.

Fortunately, research shows that as people become more competent, their assessment of their own work becomes more accurate.[5] As learners' competence increases, their overconfidence and inaccuracies decrease. The same applies to students. As they gain more feedback, insight and knowledge, they improve their ability to analyse areas where they need to improve.[6] They begin to recognize their shortcomings and learn what they do not know. They adjust their expectations and become more accepting of tuition. It is also possible that in teaching your staff to overcome their deficiencies, your workers may develop confidence in their ability to overcome problems. This builds resilience that enables them to overcome future problems they encounter in the workplace.

Schemas are also important to help our workers learn. If we understand the mental views our staff hold, we can tailor our training so that it is less likely to encounter resistance. Our existing mental models strongly affect how we interpret new information about that subject. Three different processes have been identified in how schemas affect learning. The first is accretion, where learners take the new information and incorporate it in to their schema. However, if the new information is inconsistent with what we previously believed, we may have to adjust our schemas. This is referred to as 'tuning', and is not uncommon, as our schemas frequently change as we go through life. However, sometimes the new information is so different to our pre-existing world view that we have to overhaul our way of thinking. Psychologists refer to this as 'restructuring'.

---

4   Ferraro, P.J. (2010). 'Know Thyself: Competence and Self Awareness'. *Atlantic Economic Journal*, 38(2), 183–96.
5   Ibid.
6   Kennedy, Lawton and Plumlee (2002).

One of the academics best known for promoting the link between learning and performance is Peter Senge.[7] Senge recognized that the rate at which organizations learn is an important source of competitive advantage. With this in mind, he stated that the leader's task 'is designing the learning processes whereby people throughout the organization can deal productively with the critical issues they face, and develop their mastery in the learning disciplines'.

Senge was not the first to note the link between learning and productivity. The learning curve has long illustrated this link (see Figure 4.1). It illustrates that as an organization and its workers learn more about operations, their costs decrease and productivity increases. Senge's work gave learning a new importance. He defined a *learning organization* as one 'that has developed the capacity to continuously learn, adapt and change'.

The concept of a learning organization also fitted in with the need for quality control. In a learning organization, a mistake is not an opportunity to blame, but an opportunity to learn. Growing from this is the idea of *knowledge management*. In a learning organization, employees practise knowledge management by continually acquiring and sharing new knowledge, and are willing to apply that knowledge in making decisions and performing their work. To achieve this, managers must deliberately manage their company's knowledge base. This involves the development of a learning culture where workers systematically gather and share knowledge to improve performance.

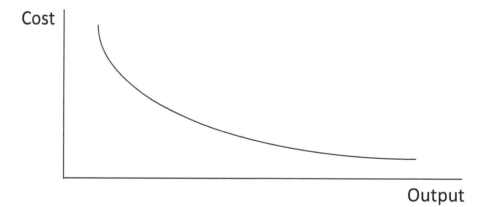

Figure 4.1   The learning curve

7   Senge, P.M. (1990). *The Fifth Dimension: The Art and Practice of the Learning Organization*, New York: Currency Doubleday.

The concept of the learning organization is not without its critics. It has been criticized for maximizing the benefits to the company without paying sufficient attention to the learning benefits for employees.[8] Critics claim that such schemes are introduced to extract higher productivity. They are controlling devices that delude workers into becoming organizational men and women.[9]

Attempts to enhance industrial learning can be undermined by union–management relations. Bratton (2001) studied attempts to enhance workplace learning in the Canadian pulp and paper industry, and found that workers perceived the learning of new skills as a threat to job security and control.[10] This presents a paradox, as workplace learning should actually increase worker flexibility and employability. But this study revealed that workers felt so threatened that they walked off the job. In this instance, there was an attempt to increase multi-skilling – for example, a pipe fitter would learn how to do some tasks normally done by welders. This blurring of job boundaries meant that other people would learn how to do their jobs, and they realized that this could undermine job security. It also impacted on normal union roles, conditions of work and wages. The situation was made worse by poor relations between the workers and managers – an illustration that learning is not value-free and that we must consider the political situation.

However, other studies have shown more positive outcomes. For example, Chang and Lee (2007) studied knowledge workers in Taiwan, and found that the implementation of a learning organization actually enhanced the job satisfaction of workers.[11] It was described as having a significantly positive effect. Similarly, a study of Greek fast-food workers found significant benefits for employees from a focus on learning.[12] When supervisors communicated how well the workers were performing and suggested ways to do better, employees felt an increased sense of optimism and became more engaged in their jobs. Daily coaching by supervisors increased the workers' engagement with their jobs and enhanced financial performance. The findings suggested

8   Nyhan, B., Cressey, P., Tomassinin, M., Kelleher, M. and Poell, R. (2004). 'European Perspectives on the Learning Organization'. *Journal of European Industrial Training*, 28(1), 67–92.
9   Sennett, P. (1998). *The Corrosion of Character: The Personal Consequences of Working the New Capitalism*. New York: W.W. Norton.
10 Bratton, J.A. (2001). 'Why Workers are Reluctant Learners: The Case of the Canadian Pulp and Paper Industry'. *Journal of Workplace Learning*, 13(7/8), 333–43.
11 Chang, Su-Chao and Lee, Ming-Shing (2007). 'A Study on Relationship among Leadership, Organizational Culture, the Operation of Learning Organization and Employees' Job Satisfaction'. *The Learning Organization*, 14(2), 155–85.
12 Xanthopoulou, D., Bakker, A.B., Demerouti, E. and Schaufeli, W.B. (2009). 'Work Engagement and Financial Returns: A Diary Study on the Role of Job and Personal Resources'. *Journal of Occupational and Organizational Psychology*, 82(1), 183–200.

that supervisors need to set clear performance goals and provide the resources required to achieve them. This includes personal resources through training. The employees need to learn the new skills and have their beliefs enhanced concerning what they can do with the skills they possess.

In a section entitled 'Leader as Teacher', Senge identified that an important role of leaders is to create space for people to learn. However, Senge's emphasis was not so much on teaching what a leader knows, but in developing workers' ability to learn for themselves and fill gaps in organizational capacity. This book argues that many opportunities exist to enhance productivity by making better use of capabilities that already exist in an organization. However, this requires an increase in teaching ability among supervisors and managers. In order to exploit the many opportunities to increase productivity on a daily basis, consider our property manager Daryl again. He describes how he fitted a coaching opportunity into his daily activities:

> I thought I would try a bit more coaching with John today, because what comes naturally to me may never occur to him. One of the traps real estate salespeople fall into is the nervousness of what to say when you are showing an apartment to a prospective purchaser. Sometimes it is better to say nothing, than to say, 'This is the kitchen.' Of course it is the kitchen, any idiot can see it is the kitchen.

> What I am coaching into John is how to endorse the core elements that might be inducing, say, a single woman to buy an apartment. Here is an example; you've inspected the apartment and have just stepped out into the corridor; I'm leading: I stop and turn back as the apartment door is swinging closed on its self-closure arm, and I say, 'Listen to that,' and it's the loud click of the door shutting and locked. I say, 'When you live in an apartment, that is the sweetest sound you ever hear … if you're going away for the weekend, you know everything is safe and secure.'

> It's not the product we are selling; it is the benefits …. For that single woman, it is the safety and security throughout the building …. I felt this hands-on form of personal coaching had inspired and motivated John in a transformational way. I could see the light go on in his eyes.

A week later, Daryl had a chance to build on the lesson that they are not selling an apartment, but the benefits embedded in it. It also became an opportunity for John to practise what he had learned the previous week:

> *Today I have a retired couple coming in to view as prospective purchasers. With their permission, I have asked John to join us. My principal function will be to have them affirm all the reasons why they are looking at apartment living as an alternative to the accommodation they have had for the last 40 years. I want John to witness the process and learn by osmosis.*
>
> *We were sitting at a table in my office, and found they like to go away on the odd weekend, so after we inspected the apartment, I said, 'I'll leave John to do the sweet sound of the door clicking behind you.'*

The relevant point from this example is the way an opportunity to learn was found in day-to-day activity, and how John gained an opportunity to practise the lesson he had learned the week before. However, just letting him observe is a start. To capitalize fully on the opportunity, at the end of the interview, John should have been asked to consciously recall what were the key things he had learned.

This raises the question of whether managers should be teachers, given that they have not had sufficient training to do so. The answer is 'yes', but it depends on the situation and what the skill deficiency is. A teacher requires two important skill sets. The first is the skill to teach, something that many managers lack. This is one area that business schools are giving limited attention – a surprising fact given that raising capabilities is one of the key drivers of performance. The second area of expertise required is knowledge of the area being taught – something that managers do not always have.

Managers are often generalists who employ specialists to conduct productive activities. As a manager, you often do not know the skills that need to be taught. Your job is administrative, and although that provides important knowledge, it might not give you the day-to-day production knowledge a worker needs. In some cases, it might be better to bring in an outside expert, or alternatively, to delegate to senior staff within the organization. Senior staff are often in a better position to do this, and in some cases, a senior staff member may be appointed on a more permanent basis to act as a mentor.

In delegating responsibility, you need to be sure that the senior staff member has the ability to train. This may place you in a situation where you must train your staff to train. They need to be aware of the need to go through the coaching stages systematically, analysing performance and identifying performance criteria, developing listening skills and evaluation.

You need to pair your trainer and trainee carefully to reduce any personal differences that might inhibit the learning process, and it may be wise to rotate the trainee between different trainers to expose them to different styles and areas of know-how. Finally, even if you have delegated the task of training, you as manager must accept that this will be a period of reduced productivity. It is a time of learning, when some breakages may occur and material may be wasted. You as a manager must keep an eye on the long term.

On-the-job training is the most common form of tuition for non–managerial staff,[13] but the quality of such training can vary dramatically. The problem is that a senior staff member who knows their job may not be very good at communicating, let alone teaching. In fact, their knowledge may be a handicap to training. They may know the job so well that they take certain steps for granted. To them, much of the job is common sense, so they provide piecemeal instruction. In their eyes, the worker seems slow to grasp the basics – an observation the senior worker is not slow to communicate, which then deflates the new worker's confidence and motivation.

If delegating, you must consider the communication abilities of the supervisor, but in assessing their communication strengths, it is not sufficient to only think about their ability to explain. They must also have an ability to listen. They must learn to seek feedback from the worker, and once again, you must consider unintended communication. Their emotional leakages might undermine the learning process, conveying different messages to their words. Finally, you may also need to consider how likely the senior worker is to criticize.

Every day, a number of opportunities to increase productivity are wasted. By enhancing teaching skills, you can increase the diffusion of production knowledge. Managers do not need to have the full training of a teacher, but some teaching skills can help increase productivity. In the next two sections, we will provide two teaching models to explore the dynamics of staff training.

---

13 Nankervis, A., Compton, R. and Baird, M. (2008). *Human Resource Management: Strategies and Processes*, 6th edn, Melbourne: Thomson.

Training Within Industry

An early industrial training technique developed with speed of learning in mind was formalized during World War Two by the US War Manpower Commission. The battles in Europe and the Pacific required huge supplies. It was a war of production. With this in mind, a programme entitled Training Within Industry (TWI) was developed to speed up manufacturing of military products.[14]

TWI recognized that simply telling staff how to do something was not sufficient training. Their handbook states: 'Most people just don't "get it" through telling. Many operations are difficult to describe in words. Few of us can use the exact words necessary, anyhow.'

Showing a staff member how to do something might overcome these problems. TWI recognizes that showing someone how to do something can be an excellent method if done properly, but it also has limitations. Workers who observe a demonstration of a task often don't know what to look for, and miss tricky points. They see the task from the perspective of a spectator, not as a doer, and even when they do get a chance to see things from the correct perspective, they don't necessarily understand the logic behind what they are doing. People cannot always translate what they see into what they should do. Consequently, showing someone what to do, by itself, is not good instruction. To overcome these problems, TWI involved a four-step program.

STEP 1: PREPARE THE WORKER

- Put the worker at ease.

- Describe the job, and find out what the worker already knows about it.

- Get the worker interested in learning the job.

- Place the worker in the correct position.

This first stage recognizes that the state of mind a worker brings to the training can have a major impact on the learning process. If the worker feels uncomfortable or has no interest in the task, they will be less likely to learn.

---

14 Training Within Industry Service (1944). *Job Instruction: Sessions Outline and Reference Material*, Washington, DC: War Manpower Commission.

If you can find ways to pique their interest, they will have questions that the training will answer. For example, I might start a lesson by saying, 'When I started this job, I made the following mistakes.' I then describe the mistakes. This can put the worker at ease, because they learn that the teacher also made mistakes, and they become less defensive. You may even be able to follow this by asking them what are the common mistakes or difficulties they have in doing the job. If workers feel they are not being criticized, they are more likely to open up about their skill deficits. They also learn that any problems they have can be solved.

STEP 2: PRESENT THE OPERATION

- Tell, show, and illustrate one important step at a time.

- Stress each key point.

- Instruct clearly, completely and patiently, but no more than the worker can master.

In the second stage, the worker actually gets to see how the job is done. To ensure that they note each part of the job, the task is broken down in to steps. You should explain not just how to do the job, but why it is done that way. This increases the worker's understanding and increases their retention. It is also important to show them how *not* to do the job, and how workers often fall into common traps.

STEP 3: TRY OUT PERFORMANCE

- Have the worker do the job, and correct any errors.

- Have the worker explain each key point to you as they do the job again.

- Make sure the worker understands.

- Continue until you know the worker knows.

A key part of learning is that you do not just explain how to do the job, but you also let them do it. In the third step, your worker actually performs the task. An important aspect of this stage is that the worker doesn't just perform the task, they explain the key points to you. This forces them to think consciously about what they are doing, as well as providing you with feedback on how well they understand the task.

Because it is their first time, they will probably make mistakes, which could be embarrassing for them. To help to create a learning culture, you could exploit this and get them to think about common ways they could make mistakes as they do the job. This shows them that identifying mistakes is an important part of the job, and also helps them to analyse and understand what they are doing. A key problem many managers face is encouraging their staff to reveal mistakes instead of hiding them.

STEP 4: FOLLOW-UP

- Put the worker on their own. Designate to whom the worker goes for help.

- Check frequently. Encourage questions.

- Taper off extra coaching, and close follow-up.

The last stage is follow-up, which refers to ongoing training once the initial session has finished. Given your worker's limited span of absolute judgement, it may be that they feel swamped with new knowledge and some aspects are forgotten or unclear. Similarly, there may be some aspects that are explained well, but you may have skimped on others. In both cases, follow-up allows you to identify these areas that may have fallen through the cracks.

Follow-up also recognizes that learning is an ongoing process. Workers may learn the skills through training, but complete mastery requires practice. To maximize skill attainment, the worker will need ongoing feedback and advice. An important point to note about TWI is the phrase, 'If the worker hasn't learned, the instructor hasn't taught.' If your worker has not attained the necessary performance level, it is tempting to blame the worker, but it also raises serious doubts about your instruction. Feedback is as much about covering your omissions as it is about identifying the worker's weaknesses.

When new workers are employed, it is common to place the recruits on a staff training course. One of the key problems with such training is that it might be another two months before they put that training into practice. In that time, they can forget much of what they were taught. Another key aspect is to recognize that each worker will have their own limited span of judgement, so bombarding them with too much information may undermine the amount of knowledge being retained. These issues confirm the need for ongoing feedback and support.

TWI training was designed for physical manufacturing processes, but the underlying logic can also be applied to service industries. Key features include not just showing them, but explaining why something is done that way, getting them to do the job, and recapping the key points they have learned. This deepens the worker's understanding of the job.

One of the things you will discover is that people have different styles of learning. Researchers have revealed specific learning types. They include *kinaesthetic learners*, who learn best by doing a task. Others may be *aural learners*, who learn best by hearing, responding well when told how to do something. Finally, there are *visual learners*, who respond best by being shown something. One of the beauties of TWI training is that it caters for all learning styles. The worker is told what to do and why, then shown what to do, then finally the worker has the chance to perform the task.

Coaching

Not all learning opportunities require structured and formal instruction, but it is important to understand the logic behind this process to overcome learning barriers in even the quickest training session. Of course, performance is not just about skill acquisition, and this highlights the difference between teaching and coaching. In teaching, the emphasis is on upgrading skills and knowledge, but this is only part of what affects performance, as shown in Figure 4.2.

Coaching takes a broader view to staff training, but nevertheless has some similarities to TWI. Both require the acknowledgement of a gap between existing performance and desired performance. In both cases, you need to identify the skills to be developed, you need to prepare the learner, present the skill, get the learner to perform the operation, and you need to follow up and evaluate. However, coaching offers a more complete approach to improving performance. Not only does it raise skills and knowledge, it also seeks to maintain motivation and ensures that organizational support and resources are in place to help employees perform at their best.

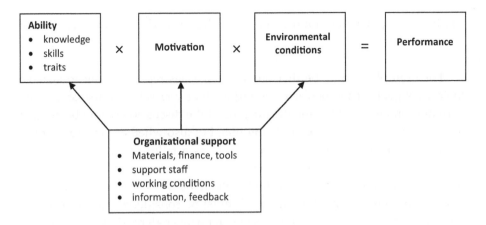

Figure 4.2   Factors that influence performance

Once again, this places demands on managers, who must enhance their own capabilities and develop the ability to coach. The skills required include teaching skills as well as analysis skills that enable you to analyse performance and the factors influencing it. You also need to develop listening skills so that you can hear how the worker perceives the situation. You must put as much effort into listening as you do talking. Finally, you will need explaining skills so that you communicate in a manner that the worker understands.

So how do you coach, and what do you do if you want to enhance your workers' performance? The four-stage coaching framework below comes from Zenger and Stinnett (2010).[15]

STAGE 1: FRAME THE CONVERSATION

Set the context for the conversation by agreeing on the purpose, process and desired outcomes of the discussion. This includes identifying the behaviour or issue to discuss, and determining the purpose or outcomes of the coaching session.

This first stage has many similarities to the first step of TWI training. The focus is on creating the preconditions for effective learning. It identifies exactly what the coaching session hopes to achieve in such a way that the person being

---

15 Zenger, J.H. and Stinnett, K. (2010). *The Extraordinary Coach: How the Best Leaders Help Others Grow*, New York: McGraw-Hill.

coached recognizes the importance of the lesson and becomes receptive to what will follow.

For example, it may be that one of your sales reps is failing to achieve their sales goals. They perceive the targets that you set as unrealistic in the current economy. In this case, the purpose of the discussion would be not just to determine why goals are not being met, but also whether your sales goals are feasible. If the problem is defined only as a failure to meet sales goals, the coaching session will be dominated by the boss's view and be seen as a mechanism for the boss to impose their will on the worker. This can reduce the worker's buy-in, so a broader approach must be considered. As a coach, you must think beyond your own perspective to uncover all barriers to learning.

STAGE 2: UNDERSTAND THE CURRENT STATE

Explore the current state from the coachee's point of view. Expand the coachee's awareness of the situation to determine the real coaching issue:

- Understand the coachee's point of view.

- Determine the consequences of continuing on the current path.

- Offer your perspective (if appropriate).

In this second stage, the sales rep has the opportunity to explain why they do not believe they can meet the goals. It may include their assessment of the market's potential and an explanation of their sales methods. This gives you a chance to identify areas for improvement. You can analyse the logic behind the goals and whether they are realistic.

You need to be aware of 'self-limiting beliefs' – thoughts, expectations and beliefs that the rep brings to the issue. Such beliefs are revealed in comments like 'I can't do this,' or 'They won't co-operate.' One of the reasons your sales rep might believe that the sales goals are unrealistic is because they have never done it before. By definition, your coaching is trying to raise their skills to a new level.

As a coach, you will need to gain an understanding on how the sale rep perceives the situation, and this places an emphasis on your listening skills. You must ask your worker how they feel about the issue. Let them describe their thoughts and feelings. The more you listen, the more you learn and the greater the opportunity to come up with an effective strategy. You must strive to listen and control your natural response to say something. It is possible that you may be disappointed by some of the things the rep says, so you must watch your body language and note any emotional leakages that could undermine the session.

STAGE 3: EXPLORE THE DESIRED STATE

Articulate the vision of success in this scenario, and explore multiple alternative paths before prioritizing methods to achieve this vision.

Having listened to and analysed the information, you must now examine what is the desirable and realistic goal, and explore with your sales rep the different ways to achieve it. You can draw upon your experience to identify different approaches your rep can try. Unlike TWI, whose emphasis is on improving skills, coaching requires an analysis of all factors affecting performance. For example, it may require you to modify the incentive system to one that is more attractive to your rep and will motivate them to try harder. It may be that some change in organizational backup is required.

STAGE 4: LAY OUT A SUCCESS PLAN

Identify the specific, time-bounded action steps to be taken to achieve the desired results, and determine milestones for follow-up and accountability.

In the last stage, you identify all the required changes and sub-goals that need to be implemented to achieve the goals. You develop a plan, including the timescale within which these activities are meant to be achieved. As with TWI, you will need to include regular follow-up sessions. Your sales rep may come across situations in which, for example, a potential client wants something slightly different to the product or service you offer. This may require a sales approach that the rep has never tried before, or alternatively, it may require a slight modification to your product offering.

Coaching is an activity that can strengthen the relationship between managers and staff, but once again, it depends on how it is done. Coaching gives you an opportunity to show that you care about their performance and want to help them, but it can also appear that you are doing it for your benefit to improve the output of your work unit. For a productive coaching relationship, you must recognize the importance of keeping feedback constructive, not negative. Any criticism should focus on the behaviour, not the person.

Knowing of your availability to help them can help create a co-dependent relationship that is positive and productive. However, in the same way that your worker will only gain skills with practice, the same applies to you as a manager and coach. Your initial attempts may not be the most successful, so you must apply the same patience and analysis skills to your own work that you would apply when coaching your workers.

What TWI and coaching have in common is a desire to meet a performance shortfall. Coaching may be more appropriate when performance is more complex and there are a number of ways to perform the task.

One of the problems you will face as a manager is knowing when to give training and instructions. If you intervene too much, the worker may think you are patronizing. However, if you don't act, you can miss out on a chance for improvement. It is another one of those balancing acts that at times you may get wrong as you develop expertise in reading the situation. We normally believe that experienced people do not need training, but that is not always the case. Consider this report from the manager of a small town council:

> *In the last few weeks, I have been inducting a new Graphic Designer into our team. He's very young with lots of talent, but little workplace experience ... I can see that I have made the mistake at times of treating him the same as his more experienced colleagues. What he's needed is more structure to his tasks, more directive leadership and less ambiguity around the way things are done. By leaving too much room for his input, he's been uncertain if what he's doing is right. This uncertainty de-motivates him and causes him to doubt the quality of what he's producing.*

> *To contrast the example above, our finance manager is very experienced, is older and needs little explanation of what's required. He's extremely competitive, self-motivated and sets high standards for himself and others. As he's an experienced accountant, I made the presumption from the outset he'd need little direction from me. Looking back, I can now see that I needed to spend more time explaining the way we want things done. I should have helped clarify for him what his experience and accounting processes would look like in our context.*

Sometimes a worker's performance has underlying problems that coaching cannot overcome. It may be that the employee is experiencing difficulties at home that are affecting their job. However, it is important to recognize the boundaries of your job, and the boundaries beyond which a worker might not want you to encroach. In addition, problems at home are likely to be outside your expertise, or alternatively, be so entrenched that you get sucked into a problem you cannot solve. As a manager, your focus is on workplace performance. Not surprisingly, most managers do not want to hear the details of an employee's private life. However, if problems are affecting work, managers can help employees realize how they are affecting their employment. In some cases, you may be able to help by rearranging work while they get through any temporary problems.

Managers should not pretend to be counsellors and offer advice on such problems, and in many cases, such advice may be taken as an insult. Where professional help is needed, many organizations offer an employee assistance programme to enable staff to get the professional help they need. If your company has such a scheme, you can let workers know such options exist without suggesting that they take them up. This provides them with options without imposing yourself upon them.

Constructive Discipline

In some cases, a worker's performance may be so bad that you have to take disciplinary action. The problem is that discipline can be counterproductive. Instead of leading the staff member to improve, it may have no effect, or even lead to retaliation. Nevertheless, sometimes managers are put in positions where discipline is necessary. This is particularly so for problems such as absenteeism, alcohol or drug abuse, insubordination, theft and other dishonesty offences, and behaviour contrary to their employment contract.

If workers perceive that decision-making is just and fair, they will continue to identify with the group, and their commitment may even increase, becoming more motivated to achieve work and organizational goals. Research shows that a worker's commitment to their work and sense of identity with their group is strongly linked to procedural justice, trust in management and satisfaction with disciplinary processes.[16]

Manoeuvring through disciplinary procedures can be greatly enhanced by an understanding of human nature as presented in our model. Attribution,

---

16 Rubin, E. (2009). 'The Role of Procedural Justice in Public Personnel Management: Empirical Results from the Department of Defence'. *Public Administration Research and Theory*, 19, 125–43.

reciprocity, social comparison, self-serving bias and emotions all have a part to play in the success of the disciplinary process.

The goal of discipline is to change behaviour. One study found that discipline could help workers to accept the rules they had contravened, but it only succeeded for half those studied. Half the workers had ongoing tendencies to break the rules.[17] The reasons were related to how discipline was handled and whether the disciplined worker perceived the punishment as retribution.

The human notion of reciprocity can influence perception and eventual success. Discipline should aim to correct any tendencies in a worker to break rules, but workers often believe that discipline is not enacted for these reasons. They perceive that you are disciplining them for retribution, as illustrated by the saying 'an eye for an eye'. Workers' perception of the process has huge implications. You need to provide full explanations for any disciplinary action that are consistent with behaviour modification, and those explanations need to be supported by other actions that help them to correct their behaviour. If the discipline is seen as taking 'an eye for an eye' and driven by personal motives, it may also undermine the faith of staff in you as a manager. Your actions should be designed to encourage improvements in behaviour.

Research shows that most workers are open to steps to modify their behaviour, and they recognize the role of deterrence. However, workers do not respond well to retribution. Workers are acutely aware that managers are the arbiters of acceptable behaviour. This gives discipline a personal element, and workers may think that you are acting for personal retribution. It can also lead to questions regarding legitimacy of the rules. One study showed that workers often believed that rule enforcement was driven by their supervisor's personal motives.[18]

An important indicator of the importance of a rule is whether there is variation in its enforcement. If workers see that a manager is inconsistent in enforcing a rule, they are less likely to take it seriously, and are less likely to change their behaviour after discipline has occurred. Similarly, such a rule will not be recognized by staff if it fails to recognize the everyday realities of the workplace. If fellow workers think it is a bad rule, then imposing discipline may be counterproductive for workplace commitment and morale.

---

17 Rollinson, R., Handley, J., Hook, C. and Foot, M. (1997). 'The Disciplinary Experience and its Effects on Behavior: An Exploratory Study'. *Work, Employment & Society*, 11(2), 283–311.
18 Ibid.

The human tendency to make social comparisons is also relevant to the disciplinary process. For example, if a worker feels they have been mistreated, comparisons with those who have received harsher treatment can make them feel that the discipline process is fair.[19] In contrast, if a worker feels they have been treated more harshly than others, they will be less likely to respect the process, and this will affect their ongoing commitment.

The way you deal with this issue has broader implications. Other workers will hear of the process and come to their own judgements about how fair they think you are as a manager. However, it is not always the case that lenient behaviour is seen as fair. The most widely known management theory based on social comparison is Adams' Equity Theory, which states that workers consider what they put into a situation compared to what they get out, then compare this with other workers. This theory is also relevant to discipline. For example, one study revealed that independent observers would accept leniency for a worker with a good record, while violators with a bad performance record were seen as more deserving of punishment.[20]

Consistent with Adams' Equity Theory is the idea that what a worker gets out of work should be consistent with what they put in. Consequently, perception of fairness of discipline depends on the nature of the discrepancy. For example, it is perceived as fair to impose discipline for theft.[21] This places you as a manager in a position to determine what level of discipline is suitable given the nature of the crime. Finding out what punishments the organization normally gives for such behaviours is a good start.

Attribution theory is particularly relevant to discipline. If a worker attributes their behaviour to external influences, they are less likely to perceive the discipline as fair. On this issue, you must be very careful, and it is appropriate to recall the two contrasting property management examples earlier in this chapter. In the first example, the staff member underperformed, but received little training or monitoring. In the second example, the staff member also made a mistake, but this time the manager attributed poor performance to his

---

19 Greenberg, J. (1988). 'Using Social Accounts to Manage Impressions of Performance Appraisal Fairness', paper presented at National Academy of Management Meeting, Anaheim, CA.
20 Niehoff, B.P., Paul, R.J. and Bunch, J.F.S. (1998). 'The Social Effects of Punishment Events: Factors that Influence Observers' Justice Perceptions and Attitudes'. *Journal of Organizational Behavior*, 19, 589–602.
21 Cole, N. (2008). 'The Effects of Differences in Explanations, Employee Attributions, Type of Infraction, and Discipline Severity on Perceived Fairness of Employee Discipline'. *Canadian Journal of Administrative Sciences*, 25(2), 107–20.

own failure to train. If a manager agrees that external factors contributed, they are more likely to be lenient – but will the manager judge their own behaviour objectively when it comes to training and monitoring?

Severity of punishment and perception of its fairness are directly linked to attribution. People believe that a discrepancy caused by the influence of external factors should receive less punishment (if any) than one they attribute to internal drives.[22] As a result, if a manager believes there were no or few external influences and solely blames the worker, the manager will apply comparatively harsh discipline. However, if the worker believes there were external forces in action, they will believe that you as manager acted unfairly.

This sort of situation could quite possibly occur given the self-serving bias that characterizes human thinking.[23] Self-serving bias can leave the worker feeling they were treated unfairly, and this has implications for whether they change their behaviour, and their ongoing sense of commitment to you and the organization. If employees consider discipline to be too harsh, it can have a significant effect on subsequent job performance.[24] This raises the importance of giving employees a chance to describe the situation fully from their position, so that any extenuating circumstances can be considered.

You as a manager will find yourself in yet another balancing act to ensure that the punishment fits the crime. You need to make sure that the punishment is consistent with that given to other workers, and consider whether the behaviour is internally or externally driven. This places the onus on you to provide clear explanations of why you have made a particular decision. One study showed that if an adequate explanation was provided, employees were 43 per cent less likely to retaliate. Explanations can also help to dampen negative emotions and reduce conflict.[25]

When imposing discipline, you may not be dealing with your normal staff member, but someone who is battling for self-esteem and has a fully aroused limbic system. And they may perceive the enemy as you. To be effective, you need to use language and act in a way that ensures you are talking to your

---

22 Ibid.
23 Ibid.
24 Ball, O.A., Trevino, L.K. and Sims Jr, H.P. (1994). 'Just and Unjust Punishment: Influences on Subordinate Performance and Citizenship'. *Academy of Management Journal*, 37(2), 299–322.
25 Bies, R.J., Shapiro, D.L. and Cummings, L.L. (1988). 'Causal Accounts and Managing Organizational Conflict'. *Communication Research*, 15(4), 381–99.

worker's neo-cortex. However, it is not sufficient to only think of the worker's emotions, but also your own. For example, it is very possible that you are angry as a result of what has happened, but you must appear calm and be aware of emotional leakages. You may make a fair comment, but if said with an angry tone, it could undermine the worker's perception of your role in the discipline process. In particular, you must monitor your non-verbal behaviour and the tone of your voice.

If presented as an opportunity for positive change, a disciplinary procedure is more likely to be effective. To achieve this, most writers stress that punishment should occur as quickly as possible after the rule has been broken. The process may be delayed, as it may take time for you to gather information, but if it is drawn out, the worker may feel that they are being made to sweat it out. This can raise resentment.[26] There is strong evidence showing how a disciplinary hearing is conducted has an impact on subsequent behaviour.[27] Managers who use a quiet, non-judgemental approach are less likely to provoke resentment from the worker.[28]

Equally important is your behaviour after the discipline has been dispensed. It is natural that you may feel continued anger or annoyance with the rule-breaking and abuse of trust, and your emotions may simmer and reignite after the disciplinary process has ended. However, if you continue to express annoyance, it could be counterproductive. You must recognize that the issue has been addressed, regardless of any residual anger you feel. The emphasis must be on behaviour, not the person. This can be very hard – after all, you have the same human characteristics as your staff. However, given the poor outcomes from disciplinary hearings, it is a difficult balancing act that you must learn to master.

Human nature covers a broad range of behavioural patterns. You may find yourself managing workers with both high and low abilities. You may have workers whose family backgrounds have given them a high degree of respect for rules and personal control, then you may have others who find this difficult. In analysing the problem, you must make a choice between focusing on the worker's attitude and ability, or considering your own performance

26 Rollinson et al. (1997).
27 Greer, C. and Labig, C. (1987). 'Employee Reactions to Disciplinary Action'. *Human Relations*, 40(8), 507–24.
28 Rollinson et al. (1997).

as manager. The former is always the easiest, but it is not necessarily the most productive.

Most people want to be successful and accepted. We have a need to belong and take pride in ourselves. A constructive approach to management focuses on helping workers to achieve these personal goals. It places the emphasis on providing clear goals and personal resources that help workers satisfy these motivations while increasing output.

5

Getting On and Having Fun

My boss had served as a Sergeant Major in the British army. He was an exceptional leader who was greatly admired by many employees.

One of the ways he built loyalty and goodwill was by looking for unexpected ways to serve his workers. On one occasion he overheard a conversation I was having with a colleague about shifting trailer loads of soil on a tight deadline. I asked for time off to do the work, which he agreed to. On a sweltering hot afternoon, as I got started shovelling this enormous pile of soil, my boss's large executive car pulls up at the address and he steps out in his trademark black pin-stripe suit. He popped open the trunk and pulled out a spade, change of clothes and a pair of gumboots. He worked alongside me all afternoon in the hot sun until the job was done.

My admiration and respect for him as a leader grew even more from that day on as he demonstrated that he was not above serving others if it served the greater good. In this way, he made it easier for his followers to 'grant him permission to lead'.

The action taken by the boss above had an element of risk. Not every worker wants to see their boss arrive at their house uninvited. Some workers like to keep a strong division between their work and home life. Secondly, some workers may feel that the manager's action left them with an uncomfortable sense of obligation that they will have to repay. However, in this case, the manager's conduct worked.

The manager's actions revealed a number of features about his leadership style. He was showing his staff that he was prepared to do extra to help them. He showed that he cared for them and was not afraid to get his hands dirty. He also showed that, in his eyes, his staff were important enough to help. Most important, the afternoon spent together sharing the hard work helped to develop a quality relationship between boss and worker.

In 2011, Ann Cunliffe and Mathew Eriksen published an article in which they criticized existing leadership theories.[1] They claimed that the leadership theories taught in business schools today do not reveal the essential nature of leadership. Cunliffe and Eriksen had studied federal security directors, and noticed that they talked a lot about relationships. They did not speak of these relationships as networks or objects, but *with people*. For example, one director stated:

> *You know, it's funny how there's always a sense of chemistry that comes from people working together and trusting each other and contributing. If you do not have that, you do not have that trust, you do not have that cooperation – then I think you are not going to be as effective.*[2]

Cunliffe and Eriksen argued for a new approach to management which they call *relational leadership*, in which leaders are sensitized to the 'importance of their relationships and to features of conversations and everyday mundane occurrences'.

Relational leaders communicate differently with their staff. For them, communication is not a time for a manager to express preconceived thoughts; it is an opportunity to let ideas and information emerge. Too many people communicate with the intention of bringing people around to their view, instead of seeing it as a chance to juxtapose ideas and create new meanings. This is what Cunliffe and Eriksen observed in their study of directors. Many of the directors they studied explicitly created space for such dialogue to occur, and allowed ideas to collide. It is an open way of working out what is possible.

However, developing relationships with staff can lead to problems. The most widely regarded theory that examines the quality of supervisor–subordinate relationships is Leader–Member Exchange (LMX) Theory,[3] which argues that effective leadership occurs when leaders and their followers develop high-quality social exchange relationships. High-quality supervisor–subordinate relationships are characterized by higher levels of mutual trust, respect and obligation.[4] In such cases, both leader and worker find they can count on one another for support and encouragement.

---

1   Cunliffe, A. and Erikson, M. (2011). 'Relational Leadership'. *Human Relations*, 64(11), 1,425–49.
2   Ibid., p. 1,432.
3   Graen, G.B. and Scandura, T.A. (1987). 'Toward a Psychology of Dyadic Organizing', in L.L. Cummings and B. Staw (eds), *Research in Organizational Behavior*, vol. 9, Greenwich, CT: JAI, pp. 175–208.
4   Sias, P.M. (2005). 'Workplace Relationship Quality and Employee Information Experiences'. *Communication Studies*, 56(4), 375–95.

In Chapter 3, we noted that it was natural for people to work well with some colleagues and not with others. If this is a human tendency, we would expect leaders to have the same bias, and this is confirmed in the early LMX research. Early studies found that managers form different types of relationships with different employees, and these relationships can vary in quality.[5] It can result in a situation where some staff are favoured ahead of others. The workplace then becomes characterized by in-groups and out-groups reflecting the boss's preference.

Those workers in the in-group enjoy high-quality exchanges with their boss. Their relationship is characterized by a high degree of mutual trust, respect and obligation. They are treated as 'trusted assistants' to the manager. In return, they perform work beyond their job descriptions. The in-group workers receive better communication and more information than their colleagues, and this gives them an advantage in terms of performance. Informed workers tend to make better decisions and contribute more to the organization.[6]

The quality of relationship with the supervisor has implications for the experience of the employee. Employees in the in-group receive better-quality information, enjoy greater autonomy and have a better relationship with the supervisor, which leads to higher job satisfaction. However, workers in the out-group experience 'low-quality exchanges' with low levels of trust, respect, and obligation. The out-group act essentially as 'hired hands' who do only what is required by their job descriptions.[7]

Having a group of trusted workers sounds desirable, but the in-group can create problems. First, it can develop into an archetypal 'yes man' situation. Secondly, it raises the problem of appearing biased. You must be very careful that you do not talk about other staff to your 'trusted' employees. You will frequently be in positions where you have to gain information from your workers, and it can be very tempting to express your personal opinion. However, it can heighten divisions among the workforce. You must always control the temptation to voice negative opinions about staff.

5   Graen, G., Dansereau, F. and Minami, T. (1972). 'Dysfunctional Leadership Styles'. *Organizational Behavior and Human Performance*, 7, 216–36; Graen, G. and Schiemann, W. (1978). 'Leader–member Agreement: A Vertical Dyad Linkage Approach'. *Journal of Applied Psychology*, 63, 206–12.
6   Sharda, R., Frankwick, G.L. and Turetken, O. (1999). 'Group Knowledge Networks: A Framework and an Implementation'. *Information Systems Frontiers*, I, 221–39.
7   Zalesny, M.D. and Graen, G.B. (1987). 'Exchange Theory in Leadership Research', in A. Kieser, G. Reber and R. Wanderer (eds), *Handbook of Leadership*, Stuttgart: C.E. Paeschel Verlag, pp. 714–27.

Those in the in-group are given higher amounts of information, influence, involvement, latitude, confidence and concern.[8] Of course, those in the out-group notice the preferential treatment of other staff. Given the human tendency to social comparison, this can have negative effects on loyalty, commitment and performance. The result can be a divided workforce, with some staff enjoying power and trust while others feel like second-grade citizens. It is preferable that all workers receive these advantages if output is to be maximized. This means that managers should be encouraged to share information with all workers, not just a chosen few.[9]

The selection of trusted employees may not be a biased process. Like all humans, we can expect managers to favour those with whom they have similarity and mutually understood common ground. Staff may also be favoured because you, as their manager, have made an objective assessment of their skills, motivation and the extent to which the worker can be trusted.[10] Managers may delegate work to staff to assess their trustworthiness, competence and ability, and find that some shine above others. Once trust is established, the manager feels less need to control the worker and can delegate to them with confidence. At the same time, the worker learns to trust their boss through a mutually reinforcing process.

In theory, employees in the out-group can break into the in-group. Because managers use delegation to assess a worker's competence, a staff member can seek greater delegation and coaching.[11] This will indicate motivation, increases skills and enhances the relationship with the boss. However, if the worker attributes the preferential treatment to personal favouritism, they might not perceive that they have the opportunity to advance, and may ignore any opportunity to do so.

Ironically, many business theories support the idea of treating staff differently. For example, situational theories of leadership suggest that leaders should treat staff differently depending on their maturity. And the theory is not without logic, as staff have different needs and require different approaches.

---

8   Dansereau, F., Graen, G. and Haga, W.J. (1975). 'A Vertical Dyad Linkage Approach to Leadership within Formal Organizations'. *Organizational Behavior and Human Performance*, 13, 46–78; Liden, R. and Graen, G.B. (1980). 'Generalizability of the Vertical Dyad Linkage Model of Leadership'. *Academy of Management Journal*, 23, 451–65.
9   Sias (2005).
10 Liden and Graen (1980).
11 Bauer, T.N. and Green, S.G. (1996). 'Development of Leader–member Exchange: A Longitudinal Test'. *Academy of Management Journal*, 39, 1,538–67.

Given the inherent logic of treating staff differently, you can find yourself conducting a delicate balancing act when finding the best way to treat your staff. The problem is made worse by time and resource constraints. Developing relationships takes time, and it is questionable how many high-quality exchanges you can profitably develop and maintain.[12]

Because of the problems that exist when a workplace is characterized by in-groups and out-groups, recent research into leader–member exchange focuses more on effective processes to develop effective leadership relationships. Instead of focusing on favoured employees, managers should provide all employees with the opportunity to develop high-quality relationships. The emphasis is on how managers may work with each person on a one-to-one basis to develop a partnership with them.[13]

In making the relationship open to all workers, the leadership process may be perceived as fairer or more equitable, and with more effective relationships, has the potential for more effective leadership and expanded organizational capability.[14] This approach has been supported by research that analysed what happens if leaders create opportunities for all staff to develop a high-quality relationship.[15] These studies revealed that those followers who accepted their leader's offer to develop a high-quality relationship improved their performance dramatically.

With the goal of generating higher-quality relationships, the Leadership Making Model was created, and once again, it is based on the idea of exchange.[16] It also explains how relationships change over time. The model describes a process in which relationships mature over time, evolving through three phases. The first is *the stranger phase*, in which leader and

12 Graen, G.B. and Uhl-Bien, M. (1995). 'Relationship Based Approach to Leadership: Development of Leader–member Exchange Theory of Leadership over 25 Years – Applying a Multi-level Multi-domain Perspective'. *Leadership Quarterly*, 6, 219–47.

13 Ibid.

14 Ibid.

15 Scandura, T.A. and Graen, G.B. (1984). 'Moderating Effects of Initial Leader–member Exchange Status on the Effects of a Leadership Intervention. *Journal of Applied Psychology*, 69, 428–36; Graen, G.B., Scandura, T.A. and Graen, M.R. (1986). 'A Field Experimental Test of the Moderating Effects of Growth Need Strength on Productivity'. *Journal of Applied Psychology*, 71, 484–91.

16 Graen, G.B. and Uhl-Bien, M. (1991). 'The Transformation of Professionals into Self-managing and Partially Self-designing Contributions: Toward a Theory of Leader-making'. *Journal of Management Systems*, 3(3), 33–48; Uhl-Bien, M. and Graen, G.B. (1993). 'Leadership-making in Self-managing Professional Work Teams: An Empirical Investigation', in K.E. Clark, M.B. Clark and D.P. Campbell (eds), *The Impact of Leadership*, West Orange, NJ: Leadership Library of America, pp. 379–87.

follower first come together, normally because one of them has just got a new job. At this stage, they do not know each other and are effectively strangers, so interaction is on a formal basis. Exchanges between the two are purely contractual. The leader only provides the follower with what is needed to do their job, while the follower behaves only as required as per their job description.

At some time during this early interaction, an opportunity arises to improve the relationship. Perhaps one of the parties offers to improve the relationship through some kind of social exchange. Alternatively, a favour may be asked for or offered. If this opportunity is accepted, the relationship moves to the second stage of relationship development: *the acquaintance stage*. They begin to get to know each other better on a personal and work level, and there is an increase in social exchanges. They begin to share more information and resources, but the exchanges are limited as they test each other out and learn whether the other person is willing to return favours.

In time, the relationship grows to the next phase, where they have *mature partnership* exchanges. This is the desirable leadership state, as both leader and follower gain greater access to resources and support from the other. The relationship is still based on reciprocity with mutual trust, respect and obligation, and they begin to share a common motivation to meet organizational goals. At this stage, workers are prepared to go beyond their job descriptions and exert extra effort. They will take personal initiative, show individual leadership of their work and take risks to accomplish assignments.[17]

This model is based on the idea that mature relations underlie effective leadership and enhance productive outcomes. There is a lot more give and take – an expression that recognizes that the relationship is still based on exchange. In fact, we could describe this evolution as one in which the quantity and quality of exchanges grows.

Many people may feel uncomfortable with an exchange-based approach to relationships. In fact, exchange-based leadership theories have been criticized by many academics. Leadership theories based on exchange are known as *transactional theories*, and have been seen as inferior to transformational leadership, where workers move beyond self-interest to a broader interest and alignment with organizational goals. In contrast, transactional leadership

---

17 Zalesny and Graen (1987).

is normally based on material exchange, in which the workers receive material rewards for their work. It is the type of work relationship we see in the first phase of this leadership model. However, this model explains how transactional leadership can evolve into a transformational relationship. As strangers learn more about each other, they begin to think beyond themselves, and the leadership evolves into something more transformational.

The final phase is still based on exchange. However, it is no longer a material exchange, but a broader social exchange with psychological benefits or favours (for example, approval, trust, esteem, support, consideration). To truly understand this process, we need to return to the model of human nature set out in Chapter 2 and recognize that humans are not just motivated by material resources, but a number of other factors such as self-esteem, security and belonging. It is these that are exchanged in transformational leadership, and lead to greater fulfilment for both the worker and manager.

Relationships between Workers: Do You Want Your Workers to Become Friends?

We could argue that it is none of your business whether your staff become friends or not. What they do in their spare time and any feelings they develop are beyond the control of managers. However, relationships between workers are important, and can have an impact on the work of a manager.

There are significant benefits if your workers develop friendships. Staff are more likely to help and mentor each other, which can increase productivity.[18] Because workers have knowledge and understanding about the workplace, co-workers are an important source of emotional and instrumental support. If workers are friends, they will obtain that support more easily and more often than those who are not. Friends can turn to each other for help. Less time is lost through conflict, and friendships can provide a buffer at times when the job is stressful and unsatisfying. This can reduce turnover. One study of workplace relationships picked up on this effect, with one worker stating: 'there's a lot of stuff going on here that makes you want to quit, that makes you not want to be here anymore, but the friends that I met here … if ever I were to quit, it would be so hard to leave some of those …'.[19]

18 Sias, P. and Cahill, D.J. (1998). 'From Co-workers to Friends: The Development of Peer Relationships in the Workplace'. *Western Journal of Communication*, 62(3), 273–99.
19 Ibid., p. 293.

The support that friends give each other can go beyond the workplace. If colleagues become close, they may help each other to improve their personal or home lives. They may share notes on problems with teenage children or spouses. They may discuss medical and retirement options, or improve physical fitness by exercising together.[20] Friends act as a second 'set of eyes and ears' for one another. They share information that may otherwise be unobtainable.[21] When combined with workplace communication, such behaviours can have a powerful influence on workplace attitudes and behaviour.[22]

This interaction can also have negative consequences. Friends discuss a wide range of topics, including gossip and non-work-related personal issues. Gossip, often influenced by the human tendency for social comparison, can lead to situations where staff are putting each other down behind each others' backs. Problems can also occur when staff experience conflicts of interest, or when their behaviour gives rise to harassment allegations.

Ominously, some friendships can develop with anti-management sentiments. Odden and Sias (1997) found that workers are more likely to form intimate relations if their supervisor is perceived as unsupportive, unfair, untrustworthy and unwilling to recognize their accomplishments.[23] Further research supports this camaraderie in the face of problems at work. Problems in their professional and personal lives can help to forge stronger relationships as workers move from being friends to close friends.[24]

Close relationships are more likely to grow if workers perceive low levels of supervisor support, fairness and consideration. They may flourish in a problematic workplace.[25] Inconsiderate supervisors and other workplace problems draw peer co-workers into closer relationships, whose communication becomes more intimate and more frequent.[26] This can result in a situation

---

20 Lu, L. (1999). 'Work Motivation, Job Stress and Employees' Well-being'. *Journal of Applied Management Studies*, 8(1), 61–73.

21 Rawlins, W.K. (1994). 'Being There and Growing Apart: Sustaining Friendships through Adulthood', in D.J. Canary and L. Stafford (eds), *Communication and Relational Maintenance*, New York: Academic Press, pp. 275–94.

22 Kirby, E.L. and Krone, K.J. (2002). '"The Policy Exists but You Can't Really Use It.": Communication and the Structuration of Work–family Policies'. *Journal of Applied Communication Research*, 30, 50–77.

23 Odden, C.M. and Sias, P.M. (1997). 'Peer Communication Relationships, Psychological Climate, and Gender'. *Communication Quarterly*, 45, 153–66.

24 Sias and Cahill (1998).

25 Sias (2005).

26 Sias and Cahill (1998).

where workers become distant and isolated from their supervisor.[27] Of course, this may not indicate a problem with friendships – it may be a wake-up call to you that your behaviour has been inappropriate and that you need to change the way you manage your team.

Despite these negative consequences, managers seem to favour the development of friendships between their staff. Berman, West and Richter surveyed managers' attitudes, and found that although they were aware that friendships posed risks, they were more than outweighed by the rewards. Table 5.1 shows that the biggest problem was gossip, with 52.8 per cent agreeing that it was a risk. This contrasts with the 84.2 per cent who believed that friendships help employees to obtain mutual support.[28]

Table 5.1   Risks and rewards of workplace friendships

	Agree or strongly agree (%)
Rewards	
Help employees obtain mutual support	84.2
Improve the workplace atmosphere	78.3
Improve communication	76.4
Make difficult jobs better	72.3
Help employees get their job done	70.4
Further acceptance of racial differences	60.2
Increase employee productivity	57.8
Improve supervisor–subordinate relationships	42.1
Help employees get ahead	30.1
Are a source of career advancement	25.0
Risks	
Cause office gossip	52.8
Are a cause of office romances	25.7
Distract from work-related activities	17.6
Are used to excuse or condone inappropriate conduct	16.2
Undermine merit-based decision-making (e.g. hiring)	15.8
Subordinate organizational loyalty to friends	14.0
Are a threat to the line of command	7.9
Are inappropriate in most organizations	6.5
Are a threat to the authority of managers	5.6

Source: Data from E. Berman, J. West and M. Richter (2002). 'Workplace Relations: Friendship Patterns and Consequences (According to Managers)'. *Public Administration Review*, 62(2), 217–30.

---

27 Sias, P.M. and Jablin, F.M. (1995). 'Differential Superior–subordinate Relations, Perceptions of Fairness, and Coworker Communication'. *Human Communication Research*, 22, 5–38.
28 Berman, E., West, J. and Richter, M. (2002). 'Workplace Relations: Friendship Patterns and Consequences (According to Managers)'. *Public Administration Review*, 62(2), 217–30.

It cannot be expected that all workers will become friends, as individuals have little say in choosing their co-workers. Employees are primarily chosen for their skills, but in recent years, employers are increasingly considering team fit when they recruit staff. A number of factors can influence the likeliness of friendship occurring. The first is the similarity of the workers' attitudes, values and interests.[29] Demographic similarity is also important, with friendships more likely to occur between workers of similar age, gender and ethnicity.[30] Not surprisingly, workers seem to cluster into sub-groups based upon family status (for example, married versus unmarried; with children versus childless).[31]

Workplace factors can also enhance the formation of friendships, some of which can be utilized by managers. Friendships are more likely when workers share co-operative tasks, share projects and work and have perceived common ground. Through shared work processes, co-workers can grow to trust and support each other, with intimate communication and emotion. Boyd Taylor surveyed managers to discover what strategies they used to maximize the productive benefits of workplace relationships. The results are shown in Table 5.2.

Table 5.2   Strategies to improve relationships

Promoting the climate for friendship and its benefits	%
Promoting a climate of openness and friendship among staff	84.4
Encouraging employees to be friendly towards each other	83.3
Training supervisors to establish positive relationships with their employees	75.2
Encouraging employees to seek each other out for support	71.2
Acknowledging and respecting employee confidences to each other	70.4
Helping employees deal with problems of interpersonal relations on the job	70.4
Instructing managers to let employees know how they care about their needs	70.1
Training employees to establish positive relations with each other	68.8
Providing opportunities for employees to socialize	66.9
Ensuring that work retreats include social activities	48.4
Providing examples of appropriate friendship relations among employees	34.6
Helping employees with similar interest to meet each other	27.8
Addressing possible risks/downsides of friendships	
Ensuring managers avoid favouritism in compensation and rewards	89.8
Training supervisors to avoid the dangers of playing favourites	81.3
Ensuring that friends of job candidates are not involved in selection processes	81.2

---

29 Lott, A.J. and Lott, B.E. (1974). 'The Role of Reward in the Formation of Interpersonal Attitudes', in T.L. Hutton (ed.), *Foundations of Interpersonal Attraction*, New York: Academic Press, pp. 171–92; Lott, B.E. and Lott, A.J. (1960). 'The Formation of Positive Attitudes toward Group Members'. *Journal of Abnormal and Social Psychology*, 61, 408–12.

30 Ibarra, H. (1993). 'Personal Networks of Women and Minorities in Management: A Conceptual Framework'. *Academy of Management Review*, 18(1), 56–87.

31 Kirby and Krone (2002).

Ensuring that friends of employees are not involved in awards processes	72.0
Eliminating the appearance or reality of good old boy/girl networks	69.2
Making supervisors alert to the dangers of cliques forming in the workplace	43.9
Reminding employees that work time must only be used for work	39.9
Training employees to deal with dangers of on-the-job friendships	37.1
Informing co-workers that loyalty to the organization comes above friendship	27.5
Informing employees of the dangers of friendships beyond the work sphere	23.8
Admonishing employees about the dangers of workplace friendships	12.0

Source: Data from E. Berman, J. West and M. Richter (2002). 'Workplace Relations: Friendship Patterns and Consequences (According to Managers)'. *Public Administration Review*, 62(2), 217–30.

In 1999, a Gallup study of 400 companies revealed the 12 most powerful indicators of a productive workforce.[32] One of the most powerful was the ability of workers to form 'best' friendships at work. Those workplaces where a worker had a best friend were most likely to have low turnover and high customer satisfaction, productivity and profitability. All in all, the literature suggests that managers should consider policies that enhance the formation of more collegial co-worker relationships. Friendships can grow from early interactions as workers develop mutual respect or need. However workers will vary in the extent to which they buy in to the process.[33]

You cannot expect workers to always get on with each other. Relationships rarely develop in a smooth or linear fashion, and tend to oscillate between the good and bad. Workplace relationships are not one-dimensional, and at times they may come under pressure. Friends can experience periods of envy, competition or neglect. Some workers may even develop feelings of physical attraction. Some relationships can become so bad that they become destructive. Berman, West and Richter (2002) state: 'It is unclear whether organizations can or should have any impact on overcoming these challenges to friendship, but they may assist through training that emphasizes active listening, the appropriateness of expressing thoughts and emotions, and acknowledgement of others' feelings.'[34]

Given the benefits of friendships, one might think that managers should strive to make work as enjoyable as possible, but how far do you go? The rest of this chapter and the next will focus on aspects of workplace relationships that can be two-edged swords, requiring managers to perform subtle balancing acts.

---

32 Shellenberger, S. (2000). 'An Overlooked Toll of Job Up-heavals: Valuable Friendships'. *Wall Street Journal*, 12 January, B1.
33 Berman, West and Richter (2002).
34 Ibid., p. 219.

Fun and Humour at Work

There has been little academic research into fun in the workplace, and there is some uncertainty whether it even belongs at work. Some writers argue that humour can distract attention from work and hinder productivity, and some forms of humour can actually upset workers. When humour is used to tease co-workers or is inconsistent with a worker's values, they may feel alienated. Some forms of humour – for example, sexual and racial jokes – run the risk of incurring legal repercussions.

On the other hand, other writers argue that fun and humour help to create an enjoyable work culture. This increases job satisfaction and reduces absenteeism and turnover, which in turn boosts productivity. Some believe that managers should actually encourage the development of a fun workplace, but once again, there is not total agreement about this. Companies attempting to introduce a 'fun or play culture' may make their workers feel manipulated by artificial attempts to impose such a culture on them. Fleming (2005) studied such 'fun cultures', in which companies tried to make work a more humorous place.[35] He discovered that many workers felt patronized, and that the fun initiatives were seen as phoney. The result can be cynicism and distaste. Some workers prefer their workplace to be dignified and respectful.

Organizations can be boring, stressful places to work, suggesting that at times, humour can play a positive role.[36] The few studies that have been carried out suggest fun can contribute to improved performance, job satisfaction and employee engagement.[37] However, the effect depends on the individual. What one person finds amusing, another may find offensive, and it is the manager who is left to find an appropriate balance. In many cases, it seems to be a question of how the humour is conducted and its suitability to the existing culture, as James Fatt of Singapore's Nanyang Technological University states: 'If used well, humor can be enjoyable and productive, when used inappropriately or poorly it can detract and have negative impacts.'[38] To understand the role of

---

35 Fleming, P. (2005). 'Worker's Playtime? Boundaries and Cynicism in a "Culture of Fun" Program'. *Journal of Applied Behavioral Science*, 41(3), 285–303.
36 Fineman, S. (2003). *Understanding Emotions at Work*, London: Sage.
37 Karl, K. and Peluchette, J. (2006). 'Does Workplace Fun Buffer the Impact of Emotional Exhaustion on Job Dissatisfaction? A Study of Health Care Workers'. *Journal of Behavioral and Applied Management*, 7(2), 128–41; Karl, K., Peluchette, J., Hall, L. and Harland, L. (2005). 'Attitudes toward Workplace Fun: A Three Sector Comparison'. *Journal of Leadership and Organizational Studies*, 12(2), 1–17; Newstrom, J. (2002). 'Making Work Fun: An Important Role for Managers'. *SAM Advanced Management Journal*, 67(1), 4–10.
38 Fatt, J.P.T. (2000). 'When Business Can be Fun', *Management Research News*, 25(1), 39–48.

humour in the workplace, we need to first understand why we humans are affected by it. There are three main theories of humour.[39]

INCONGRUITY THEORIES

These theories state that we laugh because we have an expectation of what should happen, and when it doesn't, it can be amusing. Many comedians use incongruity theory in their jokes. When telling a joke, they create an expectation, then they suddenly change it in a way that is not expected. That change is called the punch line. It surprises the audience, who laugh in response.

For example, one IT company had a clock in its workplace which told the time as any other clock did, but with one difference. Instead of chiming on the hour, the clock let out a fart noise, much to the amusement of the staff. Incongruity humour works when there is a discrepancy between what is expected to happen and what happens – the bigger the discrepancy, the bigger the joke.[40]

RELIEF THEORIES

These state that humour occurs because it releases suppressed or repressed feelings. Consider, for example, a workplace in which a number of staff have been told they are about to lose their jobs. One of the workers attempts a joke by saying, 'Is this a good time to ask for a pay rise?' The other workers laugh. To some extent, they laugh because the situation is incongruous. They didn't expect someone to ask for a pay rise once they had lost their job. However, there is another element to this form of humour. The attempt at a joke helped to release tension in what was a very intense situation.

Relief theories say that humour offers a release for pent-up emotions. Humour becomes a safe outlet for emotions that could otherwise lead to more destructive behaviour. It acts like a safety valve. For the worker, it can help remove the sense of threat and make some intolerable situations bearable.

SUPERIORITY THEORIES

The last group of theories can be linked to that ever-present human tendency to social comparison. It is the sort of humour that you often see on television

---

39 Plester, B. (2008). 'Laugh Out Loud: How Organizational Culture Influences Workplace Humor', unpublished PhD thesis, Albany, New Zealand: Massey University.
40 Ibid.

programmes like *America's Funniest Home Videos*, in which many people perform stunts that go wrong and end up hurting themselves. We laugh at another person's misfortune because at that instant, we are not unfortunate. We can enjoy a momentary feeling of superiority.

Superiority theories often involve the debasement or degradation of another person, and for that reason, can be very destructive. It is laughter at another person's expense, and this humiliation can cause much damage in the workplace.

Each of these three theories claims that humour is based on a different premise, but there is often an overlap, and some humour may draw on more than one. In most workplaces, jokes and humour accompany serious business talk. This does not normally create a problem unless it has sexual or racist overtones or someone is being degraded. Humour in the workplace can take a number of forms, such as:

- verbal or written jokes;

- artifacts (for example, the farting clock);

- visual jokes on noticeboards, posters and so on;

- electronic (for example, via email);

- banter;

- horseplay and practical jokes.

Horseplay and practical jokes can be unwelcome in the workplace. These are physical forms of humour that are often not welcome in the workplace because they disrupt work, can be noisy, may damage property and can pose a safety hazard. Most importantly, the humour behind horseplay often involves the humiliation of another staff member.

Banter is the 'playful exchange of teasing remarks'. It can be good-natured, and if a worker accepts the joke, it shows that they are a good sort. They can 'take a joke'. However, banter can be driven by superiority, as one worker tries to get the upper hand. That in itself might not be a problem, and it is not unusual to hear that one party 'gives as good as he gets'. However, banter can be a problem if a worker goes too far and their desire to gain supremacy exceeds the humorous effect. Banter can also be a problem if it takes place with a workmate who is not interested in reciprocating. In this case, the constant attacks can become insulting and tiresome. In some cases, the worker may just tolerate it and not want their boss to intervene, but in some cases they may feel bullied. The fact that everyone is laughing can make it harder for them to say something in case they are perceived as being weak or a 'poor sport'. In such situations, managers may again find themselves in a balancing act. You may not be aware of the worker's displeasure, nor whether they want your intervention, in which case you may need to talk to them to see how they feel.

Workplace humour is often aimed at a target, and frequently management is that target. You may find yourself in an uncomfortable situation when someone throws you a 'light-hearted insult'. You may challenge the worker, only to be told, 'It's just a joke.' In such situations, you may find yourself experiencing many of the same emotions as the worker above. You may not like the humour, but you don't want to appear a bad sort who ridiculously guards your authority. Nor do you want to be perceived as a boss who can't take a joke, but nevertheless, you are being insulted. Once again, you find yourself in a subtle balancing act.

Humour against management is not always 'just a joke'. It can be offensive and subversive. Humour 'can minimize status differences between leaders and subordinates', and managers may dislike the superiority aspect. However, it may be that your workers are telling you that your behaviour has gone beyond what they believe acceptable. Alternatively, the humour may be based on relief theories, in which case the workers are tolerating your actions, but using humour to vent frustration or anxiety. There are times when you will have to make unpopular decisions, and in such situations, the humour can make the decision more bearable, in which case you may need to turn the other cheek.

Humour can enable workers to express 'displeasure about facets of work to managers without the risk of reprisals'.[41] It may be just a joke, but it may also contain true or serious elements, and the humour enables staff to relax around the issue. On the other hand, the humour may express aggressive or subversive attitudes.

Managers need to be careful in responding to jokes that attack them. You will have to consider the situation and the extent to which the joke was aimed to hurt. It may be that your workers are telling you something about your

---

41 Ibid.

behaviour that you need to change. On the other hand, they may be attacking your authority. You may find that different workers laugh for different reasons. Some staff may be laughing for relief – they don't like your policy, but accept it – while others may be driven by more subversive motives. As in all situations of attribution, managers have to be very careful when attributing the motives of the joke-teller.

A manager might want to show they are a good sort by reciprocating and making a joke at the expense of the person who made the initial joke. However, this can backfire if it leads to ongoing banter. Such participation may also limit your future options if you want to bring an end to the humour. If you do feel a worker has gone too far, it is best to say something in private, and let the joke-teller know it was inappropriate in a manner that protects their self-esteem and doesn't undermine your relationship – a gentle word.

Much of what is considered appropriate is determined by the workplace culture. Barbara Plester at Auckland University studied the cultures of four companies, and discovered wildly different approaches to humour.[42] The companies included a medium-sized law firm, a small IT service company, a large financial services company and a large utilities company. Each of these had a very different culture and a different approach to humour.

The first company studied by Plester was Kapack, a medium-sized law firm which claimed to have a fun culture, but the reality was very different. The company had strict boundaries, particularly with regard to noise and the potential for fun to be distracting. One staff member explained:

> We need to have young people and we need to have fun, but I still worry
> a little bit when they get a little bit too loud and laughing too much that
> it is not quite professional and it might look like perhaps that they are
> not doing much to other people.[43]

In this company, electronic forms of humour were scanned for offensive or inappropriate material by IT staff. Humorous video files were deleted, and only work-related video files were permitted. This legal firm was clearly aware of the legal implications of such humour: 'It is a work environment, and now with harassment and the way employment is – you have to be very careful

42 Ibid.
43 Plester, B. (2009). 'Crossing the Line: Boundaries of Workplace Humor and Fun'. *Employee Relations*, 31(6), 584–99, p. 589.

what you say to people and how you say it ... and I think that has put a little bit of a dampener on humor.'[44]

The second company studied by Plester was Sigma, a large financial company with clear boundaries for fun and humour. Although there were no official rules, the staff knew what behaviours were appropriate. The employees interviewed by Plester used phrases like 'going too far' or 'crossing the line' – comments that recognized definite boundaries. This included physical jokes that risked bodily harm and humour promoting prejudice, sexism or concerned sexual matters. Such humour could create disharmony, as one staff member noted: 'People are fairly careful with inappropriate humor ... people understand that they don't want to put people out too much so they are reasonably careful about what kinds of humor they apply.'[45]

If that line was crossed, managers performed a gate-keeping role. For example, Plester observed one staff member say loudly 'For f***'s sake!' in order to make her colleagues laugh. Her manager recognized the line had been crossed and responded by saying. 'Oh, the mouth on you!' He said this publicly but gently, and all the staff laughed, but everyone understood that a censure had been intended and the boundary reinforced.[46]

In contrast to Kapack, where fun was espoused but somewhat lacking, humour was more observable at Sigma. The management seemed to perform a successful balancing act. They openly encouraged fun, but simultaneously reinforced boundaries of what was acceptable. These boundaries were clearly defined and embedded in the company culture, which made their enforcement easier for management.

The third company studied by Plester made the greatest use of humour. This was Adare, a small information technology firm with expertise in security and networking. The company was male-oriented, with only three women among the 25 staff. It was the smallest of the companies studied, and had no formal policies regarding fun and humour.

Managers at Adare did not enforce boundaries as they did in other companies. In fact, there appeared to be no boundaries. The company's

---

44 Ibid.
45 Ibid., p. 592.
46 Ibid.

managing director was an enthusiastic joker, and his personality shaped the company's culture. He initiated much of the humour, the nature of which seemed to have no limits. For example, on one occasion, a staff member returned to the office with a potential client only to find the managing director simulating sex with another male colleague, much to the amusement of the other staff.

With a predominantly male workforce, humour in the company had a strong gender effect. Humour was a way of displaying masculinity, and was highly competitive. Victims of pranks displayed their masculinity by 'taking it' with a laugh. Much of the fun was superiority humour, with amusement gained from the degradation of another staff member. It included banter and practical jokes, and had an underlying reciprocity principle. There was a strong emphasis on 'paying people back' for pranks and insults.

In complete disregard to employment laws, many of the jokes attacked staff members' sexuality, insinuating, for example, that a male colleague is homosexual. Humour was racist and sexist, and staff took great joy at thumbing their noses at the 'politically correct' world that lay beyond the company's walls. Employees readily admitted that management could easily incur a sexual harassment lawsuit, and this meant that great care needed to be taken when recruiting and selecting staff. Workers who could not take a joke would not survive in this culture.[47]

Humour at Adare took the form of printed jokes, emails, artifacts (including a farting clock), cartoons and graffiti messages such as 'Bruce blows goats!' scrawled on one partition. Fun was often highly physical. On one occasion, a new female staff member was observed calmly talking on the phone to a customer while food was flying around her head. Staff were used to loud and unusual activities, and seemed to enjoy it, reporting: 'The culture, a lot of it has got to do with the humor that we have, we all share the same sort of idiotic behavior,' and 'The humor is the culture. We love humor, we love laughter.'[48]

Staff at Adare were proud of their fun culture and their difference to other IT companies. Through humour, employees developed a high sense of identity with their organization, giving the company high staff retention rates. Employees knew they would not be able to behave the same and have as much fun at other companies. One staff member noted:

47 Plester (2008).
48 Plester (2009), 590.

This organization is like nothing you have ever come across. Most people who come and visit us are just taken completely aback by how open the place is, how dry and perhaps risky, the humor is. Some places are so politically correct that you can't say boo, if you take this as anti-PC, this is exactly what the place is like, which is great.[49]

Humour in this company seemed to have no limits. However, two women administration workers created their own personal boundaries. They firmly told the men 'that should they be physically touched during any fun activities a bottle of wine must be provided in compensation'.[50] The men respected their boundaries and did not include the women in physical jokes. However, the only other female staff member, a sales employee, participated fully and appeared to have become 'one of the boys'.

The last organization in Plester's study was Uvicon, a large utility company supplying electricity and gas. As at Sigma, employees at Uvicon were sensitive to the fact that some forms of humour can create negative feelings. Staff wished to maintain a careful and caring culture, and were uncomfortable with humour that could cause offence. Sarcasm was looked down upon, and there was no tolerance of sexual or racist jokes. The gate-keeper role was seriously maintained, and staff were reprimanded for inappropriate humour: 'We haven't got destructive humor and if we do see destructive humor [such as sarcasm] we point it out and it is not going to be positively received.'[51]

On one occasion, a company joker hid inside a large plastic rubbish bin and jumped out in an attempt to surprise his colleagues. However, he was unofficially reprimanded by the HR manager, who suggested that such pranks could harm employees with heart problems. The joker accepted that he had crossed boundaries, and stated he would not attempt similar jokes in the future.

However, there seemed to be different attitudes to humour within the company. In the engineering department, a similar prank was observed without any repercussions. On this occasion, an engineer silently crept up behind a colleague, then suddenly surprised him with a loud noise while dropping his hands on his shoulders. The colleague shouted with fright, to the amusement of nearby staff, who laughed and made further quips. Unlike the HR department, the engineering department accommodated such humour. The concern for

---

49 Ibid., p. 591.
50 Plester (2008).
51 Plester (2009), 594.

harmony, so prevalent in other departments, did not exist here. It was the only department in the company where jokes and cartoons were displayed on the walls and staff openly told sexual, sexist and racial jokes.

In all four companies studied by Plester, the culture influenced what was considered appropriate. Boundaries were created by people within the organization, and were influenced by the level of formality, size of company, the industry, gender, and in the case of Adare, the personality of the managing director. Common boundaries included sexual or racist humour, jibes targeted at personal characteristics, physical jokes and humour that was noisy or distracted from work.

People learned the boundaries over time through the socialization process, and sometimes by making mistakes. As part of that learning process, managers might have to advise staff what was appropriate. However, management intervention was often not required, as other staff spoke to their colleagues. Staff also learned that boundaries may vary depending on the time and context. On some occasions, they might get away with behaviours that on others would be considered 'going too far' and 'crossing the line'. Boundaries are dynamic and shaped by different humorous and cultural events. In any organization, there may be different values among the staff, and this may lead to disagreements as to where the boundaries lie.

Plester states that humour is very dependent on who does it. In some organizations, an employee may take the role of 'the joker' – a position which provides popularity and status among their colleagues. The joker can get away with behaviour that may be considered inappropriate in others: 'The joker performs some key functions within organizations such as challenging management, pushing the boundaries, developing the culture, and providing relief from stress and pressure.'[52] However, the key to being a joker is social knowledge. The joker must know the people they are making fun of, and they must know the workmates that are watching. It is this relationship that allows jokers to act as they do.[53]

Building a relationship and gaining knowledge of what colleagues tolerate and enjoy takes time. It requires a period of relational learning. Like the worker

52 Plester, B.A. and Orams, M.B. (2008). 'Send in the Clowns: The Role of the Joker in Three New Zealand IT Companies'. *Humor: The International Journal of Humor Research*, 21(3), 253–81.
53 Fine, G.A. and De Soucey, M. (2005). 'Joking Cultures: Humor Themes as Social Regulation in Group Life'. *Humor: International Journal of Humor Research*, 18(1), 1–22.

described above who jumped out of a rubbish bin, the joker may experience occasional periods when a staff member is offended and the boss needs to have a 'quiet word'. However, once the social knowledge is gained, the joker may make work a more enjoyable place to be.

Because of the need for social knowledge, smaller companies can allow riskier forms of humour. Staff have greater opportunity to get to know each other. However, in larger companies, it may take longer to become so familiar with colleagues. Larger companies are also likely to have more diverse groups of employees, and this can increase the chances that offence may be taken.

Research reveals that there are differences between the sexes. Men show a greater preference for sexual humour than women.[54] Humour helps to create masculine identity and a sense of belonging. Sexual and aggressive jokes can contribute to male bonding and improve group solidarity.[55] Men are more likely to use superiority humour,[56] and being able to take a joking insult 'is seen as a factor of group membership and a demonstration of masculinity'. They are also more likely to enjoy jokes that break societal rules – something that creates excitement and strengthens male camaraderie.[57]

On the negative side, staff may feel pressured to conform to ideals of masculinity,[58] and women working in workplaces characterized by masculine ideals may feel they have to become 'one of the boys' or risk being alienated.[59] A woman working in a male-oriented culture is in an interesting situation. To gain insight into this, reverse the situation and ask, 'Where does this place a man in a predominantly female workforce?' In this case, we would expect the man to conform, for if he told sexist jokes, he would be in danger of causing offence.

54 Duncan, J.W., Smeltzer, L.R. and Leap, T.L. (1990). 'Humor and Work: Applications of Joking Behavior to Management'. *Journal of Management*, 16(2), 255–79; Eastman, M. (1936). *Enjoyment of Laughter*, New York: Simon and Schuster.

55 Pratt, M.G. (2001). 'Social Identity Dynamics in Modern Organizations: An Organizational Psychology/organizational Behavior Perspective', in M. Hogg and D. Terry (eds), *Social Identity in Organizational Contexts*, Philadelphia, PA: Psychological Press.

56 Kehily, M.J. and Nayak, A. (1997). '"Lads and Laughter": Humor and the Production of Heterosexual Hierarchies'. *Gender & Education*, 9(1), 69–87.

57 Lyman, P. (1987). 'The Fraternity Bond as a Joking Relationship: A Case Study of the Role of Sexist Jokes in Male Group Bonding', in M.S. Kimmel (ed.), *Changing Men: New Directions in Research on Men and Masculinity*, Thousand Oaks, CA: Sage, pp. 143–53.

58 Collinson, D. (1988). 'Engineering Humor: Joking and Conflict in Shop-floor Relations. *Organization Studies*, 9, 181–99.

59 Fine and De Soucey (2005).

Similarly, we might expect a woman in a male workplace to conform. In which case, if a woman does not like humour that the men enjoy, the boss could tell her to toughen up and not be so sensitive. However, there are important reasons why a boss cannot do this. Laws in most countries prohibit sexual and racial discrimination. If a female staff member feels discriminated against, the manager has to act, or risk expensive and time-consuming litigation. While a man might find a female-oriented workplace boring and politically correct, there are no laws prohibiting boredom.

Managers must protect individual staff, and this can often be done with little effort. Like the women at Adare who created boundaries for themselves by saying they didn't want to be involved in physical pranks, managers can tell their staff to protect the boundaries of individual people. But what should be done about publicly placed humour? For example, a poster on the wall at Adare had a male standing with clinched fist over a woman who was lying on the ground. The poster read: 'Punch her in the face to show that you are right.'[60] Interestingly, none of the women at Adare found the poster offensive. The women knew the jokers in the workplace, and it seemed that none of the men actually endorsed those values. In this case, the humour was not superiority humour, but a combination of relief and incongruity humour. As relief humour, it was a vent against the politically correct world that lay outside. As incongruity humour, it was a complete break from expectations of a workplace. However, we could understand why a new female worker might find it offensive.

A strong case could be made for courts to consider culture when making decisions about offensiveness. Until then, managers must take great care in selecting and recruiting to ensure that they fit the existing culture and are fully aware of what they can expect in the job. You must respect the dignity of your workers and that means creating the necessary boundaries. However, workers also want to enjoy going to work, and this must be balanced against the need to respect staff and show professionalism. It is you, as manager, who must perform this balancing act.

---

60 Plester (2008).

6

Bullying

Duncan works as a skilled labourer in a manufacturing plant. He works in a separate unit to Jim, but occasionally he is told to help Jim out during peak workloads. This is not an experience that Duncan enjoys, as Jim always finds something to criticize about his work. For example, yesterday he criticized how Duncan maintained his tools.

Duncan explained to me, 'I have been doing this job for years and I know how to look after my tools. But it's not about the tools. It's just one example of criticism.'

Jim also likes to joke with Duncan, at least that's how Jim sees it. 'He makes these snide remarks that are meant to be attempts at banter, but there is nothing funny in it at all.'

I asked Duncan why he didn't complain. He replied by saying it wasn't a big enough issue. 'It's just tedious, really tedious. Sometimes I feel like I don't want to go in to work so I don't have to put up with it.'

Interpersonal conflicts are a regular occurrence in workplaces. Research suggests that managers spend about 20 per cent of their time dealing with conflicts.[1] These can include disputes over resources, goals or work procedures. In such cases, conflict is resolved by addressing the matter at hand, but in some cases, conflict can be very personal. In this chapter, we explore one of the more personal types of conflict – bullying.

An immediate problem with the literature is that academics do not always agree about what constitutes bullying. Einarsen defines bullying as: 'repeated acts and practices that are directed at one or more workers, which are unwanted by the victim(s), which may be done deliberately or unconsciously, but clearly

---

1   Thomas, K.W. (1992). 'Conflict and Negotiation Processes in Organizations', in M.D. Dunnette and L.M. Hough (eds), *Handbook of Industrial and Organizational Psychology*, vol. 3, Palo Alto, CA: Consulting Psychologists Press, pp. 651–718.

cause humiliation, offence, and distress, and may interfere with job performance and/or cause an unpleasant working environment'.[2] This definition identifies that bullying involves repeated negative acts that are directed at one or more people, and as a result that person feels some level of stress.

Another definition includes the victims' difficulty in defending themselves. It states that bullying is: 'a situation in which individuals persistently over a period of time perceive themselves to be on the receiving end of negative actions from one or several persons, in a situation in which the target of bullying has difficulty defending himself or herself against these actions'.[3] This may include direct acts like verbal abuse, accusations and public humiliation, or it may be indirect and take the form of gossip, spreading rumours and social exclusion.[4] It may include deliberate attacks on the worker's private life or attitudes. If the bully is a supervisor, it may include unnecessary criticism or excessive monitoring of work. A bullying boss may also withhold information, deprive staff of responsibility or give a person undesirable or overly simple tasks.[5]

These definitions focus on repeated acts, which suggests that a one-off act of aggression is not considered to be bullying. It is this aspect that differentiates between 'normal' conflict and bullying. Personal conflict and interpersonal aggressive acts may occur in the workplace for a number of reasons, but they will not be defined as bullying unless they occur as persistent and continuous behaviour. That is not to say that single acts of aggression are permissible, but they will fall under a different category of misdemeanour.

Workers exposed to bullying can end up feeling frustrated and stressed with the situation they find themselves in. They may feel a sense of helplessness and become alienated from their workplace, which in turn reduces their sense of belonging to the organization, while bullying itself will reduce work unit cohesiveness.[6] Bullying is often an attack on one of our core motives – self-esteem. The resulting shame and psychological despair can last long after the

---

2   Einarsen, S. (1999). 'The Nature and Causes of Bullying at Work'. *International Journal of Manpower*, 10, 16–27, p. 17.
3   Einarsen, S., Hoel, H., Zapf, D. and Cooper, C. (2003). 'The Concept of Bullying at Work: The European Tradition', in S. Einarsen, H. Hoel, D. Zapf and C. Cooper (eds), *Bullying and Emotional Abuse in the Workplace: International Perspectives in Research and Practice*, London: Taylor & Francis, pp. 3–30.
4   Ibid.
5   Salin, D. (2003). 'Ways of Explaining Workplace Bullying: A Review of Enabling, Motivating, and Precipitating Structures and Processes in the Work Environment'. *Human Relations*, 56(10), 1,213–32.
6   Ashforth, B. (1994). 'Petty Tyranny in Organizations'. *Human Relations*, 47, 755–78.

bullying episodes have ended.[7] The result is lower job satisfaction, which in turn increases absenteeism and turnover.

This can have a significant effect on productivity.[8] In 1990, a Swedish study attempted to quantify the costs of bullying and harassment.[9] The study included the loss of productivity combined with intervention costs, and came to an amount of US$30,000–100,000 per year (in 1990 dollars). Workers themselves recognize this cost. In a study of 2,215 Norwegian labour union members, 27 per cent claimed that productivity had been reduced because of harassment.[10]

Bullying appears to be widespread. A study of a Norwegian shipyard showed that 7 per cent of the men were subjected to personal belittlement on a weekly basis.[11] Some bullying had a strong social element. This included exposure to gossip or rumours, insulting teasing, offensive remarks or being met with silence when entering a conversation. Some were socially excluded from their work group. Other bullying was centred on the work. This included having their work efforts constantly devalued, being denied access to information needed for their job, or being repeatedly deprived of work tasks and responsibilities.

Some of these bullying acts, such as insulting teasing, show similarities to superiority humour and banter. This raises a number of possibilities. The first is that what one person considers light-hearted banter may be considered unwelcome insults by another. It also suggests that some masculine behaviours in the workplace may be destructive. There is some evidence to suggest this is the case, as many studies show males have a significantly higher probability of being perpetrators of bullying than women.[12] Tough, male-dominated work

7   Roscigno, V.J., Lopez, S.H. and Hodson, R. (2009). 'Supervisory Bullying, Status Inequalities and Organizational Context'. *Social Forces*, 87(3), 1,561–89.

8   Keashly, L. and Nowell, B.L. (2003). 'Conflict Resolution and Bullying', in S. Einarsen, H. Hoel, D. Zapf and C. Cooper (eds), *Bullying and Emotional Abuse in the Workplace: International Perspectives in Research and Practice*, London and New York: Taylor & Francis, pp. 339–58.

9   Leymann, H. (1990), 'Mobbing and Psychological Terror at Workplaces'. *Violence and Victims*, 5, 119–26.

10 Einarsen, S., Raknes, B.I., Matthiesen, S.B. and Hellesoy, O.H. (1994). *Mobbing og Harde Personkonflikter* ('Bullying and Harsh Personalized Conflict'), Bergen: Sigma Forlag.

11 Einarsen, S. and Raknes, B.I. (1997). 'Harassment at Work and the Victimization of Men'. *Violence and Victims*, 12, 247–63.

12 De Cuyper, N., Baillien, E. and De Witte, H. (2009). 'Job Insecurity, Perceived Employability and Targets and Perpetrators of Workplace Bullying'. *Work and Stress*, 23(3), 206–24; Rayner, C. (1997). 'The Incidence of Workplace Bullying'. *Journal of Community and Applied Social Psychology*, 7, 199–208.

environments may accept humiliating jokes and 'funny surprises' as part of the everyday life and an accepted part of the culture.[13] Salin (2003) observes: 'However, this kind of humor can easily go sour and turn into bullying if the target for some reason cannot defend himself or take the jokes "as a man".'[14]

While male banter may provide an explanation for some occurrences, there are many other types of bullying, and industries dominated by women and educated professionals also appear to harbour this destructive behaviour. A study of 99 psychiatric nurses and assistant nurses revealed that 10 per cent felt exposed to bullying at work.[15] In two separate surveys of American nurses, 64–82 per cent had experienced verbal abuse from physicians and supervisors.[16] Teaching is particularly notable as a profession prone to bullying.[17] High rates of bullying in the education sector have been recorded in Australia,[18] Finland,[19] the Netherlands,[20] the UK[21] and the USA.[22] In the UK, it seems that the prevalence of bullying in teaching is only surpassed by that among postal/telecommunications and prison staff.[23] Even the most intellectual and educated people seem to be involved. A survey of 726 Finnish university employees found that 24 per cent of females and 17 per cent of males experienced workplace harassment.[24]

---

13 Collinson, D.L. (1988). 'Engineering Humor: Masculinity, Joking and Conflict in Shopfloor Relations'. *Organization Studies*, 9(2), 49–67; Einarsen and Raknes (1997).
14 Salin (2003), p. 14.
15 Matthiesen, S.B., Raknes, B.I. and Røkkum, O. (1989). 'Mobbing på Arbeidsplassen' ('Bullying in the Workplace'). *Tidskrift för Norsk Psykologförening*, 26, 761–74.
16 Cox, H.C. (1987). Verbal Abuse in Nursing: Report of a Study'. *Nursing Management*, 18, 47–50; Diaz, A.L. and McMillin, J.D. (1991). 'A Definition and Description of Nurse Abuse'. *Western Journal of Nursing Research*, 13, 97–109.
17 Randall, P. (2001). *Bullying in Adulthood: Assessing the Bullies and their Victims*, New York: Brunner-Routledge.
18 Vickers, M.H. (2001). 'Bullying as Unacknowledged Organizational Evil: A Researcher's Story'. *Employee Responsibilities and Rights Journal*, 13, 205–17; McCarthy, M., Mayhew, C., Barker, M. and Sheehan, M. (2003). 'Bullying and Occupational Violence in Tertiary Education: Risk Factors, Perpetrators and Prevention. *Journal of Occupational Health and Safety Australia and New Zealand*, 19, 319–26.
19 Björkqvist, K., Osterman, K. and Hjelt-Back, M. (1994). 'Aggression among University Employees'. *Aggressive Behavior*, 20, 173–84.
20 Hubert, A.B. and Van Veldhoven, M. (2001). 'Risk Sectors for Undesirable Behavior and Mobbing'. *European Journal of Work and Organizational Psychology*, 10, 415–24.
21 Lewis, D. (2003). 'Voices in the Social Construction of Bullying at Work: Exploring Multiple Realities in Further and Higher Education. *International Journal of Management and Decision Making*, 4, 65–8.
22 Spratlen, L.P. (1995). 'Interpersonal Conflict which Includes Mistreatment in a University Workplace'. *Violence and Victims*, 10, 285–97.
23 Hoel, H. and Cooper, C. (2000). 'Destructive Conflict and Bullying at Work', unpublished report, Manchester: University of Manchester Institute of Science and Technology.
24 Björkqvist, Osterman and Hjelt-Back (1994).

These statistics raise a number of questions. First, do our teachers lack ethics given their high rate of bullying? This is an issue of concern given that they provide a moral education to our young. It also raises questions about how we teach ethics – something we will look at in Chapter 8. However, alternative explanations have focused on characteristics of teaching that might increase the chance of bullying occurring. For example, in Australia, teaching has been characterized by increasing workloads and working hours, and this increases interpersonal tension.[25] Consider the following example:

> Henry was a maths teacher in a high school where one class of 15-year-olds contained a particularly disruptive student. Whenever Henry's back was turned, books would go flying, and on one occasion a pen hit him in the back of his head. Henry found it very hard to get organizational support, but finally convinced the school principal to witness a class. The principal stood outside, out of sight of the students, but in such a position that he could see everything through a window. After a very short time, the principal had confirmed what Henry was saying about the student.

> A formal complaint was laid against the student, who responded with a counter-claim against Henry. The student claimed that Henry had been unfairly harassing him in class. Of course, the principal had seen everything, so the counter-claim should have been thrown out, but it wasn't.

> A counsellor was brought in to conduct a meeting, which included the student, his parents, Henry and the principal. The student was given a chance to speak, and made a number of false complaints against Henry. They were blatant lies, yet no one said a word.

> Finally, the principal spoke up, and the boy's parents quickly realized the truth, but the counsellor, who was keen to keep the peace, turned to the student and said, 'None of this is a reflection of you.'

> Henry was disgusted. After all he had to tolerate while teaching, followed by the false accusations, 'where was the organizational support? Where was the apology?'

---

25 Dorman, J. (2003). 'Testing a Model for Teacher Burnout'. *Australian Journal of Educational and Developmental Psychology*, 3, 35–47.

> *In a politically correct attempt to keep the peace, the counsellor had just*
> *convinced Henry that he no longer wanted to be a teacher.*

One study suggests that the nature of teacher output has an impact on the amount of bullying that occurs. In particular, it is hard to measure the quality and quantity of a teacher's work, and this increases the importance of interpersonal relationships with both colleagues and superiors in performance appraisals.[26] An imbalance of power and intense competition can increase the chances of bullying occurring. Interpersonal conflict among school teaching staff is quite common, particularly in situations where teachers are working in teams.[27]

A poor work environment does not cause bullying, but it can raise tensions and frustrations that make bullying more likely to occur. In some cases, it can increase negative emotions that spill over. In others, work design increases competition and interpersonal rivalry. A lot of research in Scandinavia has identified workplace factors that can increase the chances of bullying occurring, as explored below.[28]

REWARD SYSTEM AND WORKING ARRANGEMENTS

Some researchers have argued that individual-based reward systems may stimulate bullying, as some people may want to show that their performance is better than others.[29] This leads to negative competitive workplace behaviour. The obvious solution would be to introduce team-based reward systems, but these can themselves promote bullying, as team members may take their anger out on under-performing staff who drag the team's performance down and decrease their bonuses.[30]

JOB DESIGN

If the work itself is badly designed, it can increase tensions and competitiveness. Although management research supports the creation of work teams, it also

---

26 Hubert and Van Veldhoven (2001).
27 Main, K. (2007). 'Conflict in Middle School Teaching Teams: Friend or Foe?'. *Australian Journal of Middle Schooling*, 7, 12–16.
28 Çangarli, B.G. (2009). 'A Review of the Organizational Antecedents of Bullying'. *International Journal of Business Research*, 9(6), 100–106.
29 Neuman, J.H. and Baron, R.A. (1998). 'Workplace Violence and Workplace Aggression: Evidence Concerning Specific Forms, Potential Causes, and Preferred Targets'. *Journal of Management*, 24(3), 391–419.
30 Collinson (1988).

suggests that work requiring a high degree of co-operation and teamwork may actually increase the incidence of peer bullying. This was found in the Australian teaching study mentioned above, where teamwork actually increased interpersonal tensions. Some team members may become scapegoats for failures, and aggressive team members may focus on the least powerful group members. Using workers as scapegoats can be a result of displaced aggression, where aggression aroused by a different cause, in this case failure, is then directed at something else, in this case a staff member. Focusing aggression in this way may provide an outlet that relieves group tensions, but it is not fair on the worker being targeted.

Other features of poorly designed workplaces involve information and work control. When workers do not receive sufficient information about their job[31] and have low control over it,[32] their stress levels are increased. There is less tolerance for mistakes. If other workers or supervisors do have that information and control, it can put those people in a position of power that they can exploit. A German study revealed that workers who had control over time were less likely to be victims than those who didn't.[33] The same study revealed that reliance on others also raised the possibility of aggression. When people are forced to work closely together, it increases the chances of unresolved conflicts that can escalate into harassment.

ORGANIZATIONAL CULTURE AND CLIMATE

A number of studies have looked at the culture of organizations and found that bullying workplaces have competitive cultures, while non-bullying workplaces are easy-going and less competitive.[34] A quest for excellence can also contribute to bullying behaviour, as can be seen in the abuse doled out by some top chefs.[35]

31 Vartia, M. (1996). 'The Sources of Bullying: Psychological Work Environment and Organizational Climate'. *European Journal of Work and Organizational Psychology*, 5(2), 203–14.
32 Rayner, C., Sheehan, M. and Barker, M. (1999). 'Theoretical Approaches to the Study of Bullying at Work. *International Journal of Manpower*, 20(1/2), 11–16; Omari, M. (2003). *Towards Dignity and Respect: An Exploration of Antecedents and Consequences of Bullying Behavior in the Workplace*, final report, Curtin-IPAA Fellowship Programme, Perth: Curtain University.
33 Zapf, D., Knorz, C. and Kulla, M. (1996). 'On the Relationship between Mobbing Factors and Job Content, Social Work Environment, and Health Outcomes. *European Journal of Work and Organizational Psychology*, 5(2), 215–37.
34 Vartia (1996); O'Moore, M., Seigne, E., McGuire, L. and Smith, M. (1998). 'Victims of Bullying at Work in Ireland'. *Journal of Occupational Health and Safety: Australia and New Zealand*, 34(6), 568–74.
35 Johns, N. and Menzel, P.J. (1999). '"If You Can't Stand the Heat!": Kitchen Violence and Culinary Art'. *Hospitality Management*, 18, 99–109.

Some cultures may promote an image of toughness.[36] When group norms allow aggressiveness in social interaction, it creates an environment in which bullying and harassment can easily occur. Aggressive interaction is 'permitted', as it is the way things are done in that organization.[37] An employee may engage in bullying behaviour because there will be no punishments for doing so. In this case, managers need to balance an aggressive culture with guidelines about what the limits are. This requires a policy against bullying, active monitoring and reprimands for those who engage in bullying. If these do not exist, the organization may suffer because of the lack of restraints.

LEADERSHIP

The behaviour of managers can have an important influence on the likelihood that bullying will occur.[38] A superior who encourages competition for tasks, status or advancement can sow the seeds of interpersonal conflict.[39] Similarly, 'weak' or 'inadequate' senior leadership can enable a bully to flourish at lower levels.[40] If management does not intervene in bullying, perpetrators see no reason to change their behaviour or even think that they have done anything wrong.

While inactive management can foster bullying, so can management that is too heavy-handed. A number of studies suggest that authoritarian management styles help to foster bullying, and people working in departments with authoritarian bosses are more likely to report being bullied.[41] In some cases, the manager acts as a petty tyrant. A study by Ashforth revealed that some managers make arbitrary decisions regarding staff and show a lack of consideration to subordinates.[42] Such managers display self-aggrandizing behaviours and use force in conflict-resolution. In such cases, not only is the

---

36 Neuman and Baron (1998).

37 Salin (2003).

38 Hoel, H. and Salin, D. (2003). 'Organizational Antecedents of Workplace Bullying', in S. Einarsen, H. Hoel, D. Zapf and C. Cooper (eds), *Bullying and Emotional Abuse in the Workplace: International Perspectives in Research and Practice*, London: Taylor & Francis.

39 Leymann, H. (1996). 'The Content and Development of Mobbing at Work. *European Journal of Work and Organizational Psychology*, 5(2), 165–84.

40 Einarsen, S., Raknes, B.I. and Matthiesen, S.B. (1994). 'Bullying and Harassment at Work and their Relationships to Work Environment Quality: An Exploratory Study'. *European Work and Organizational Psychologist*, 4(4), 381–401; Hoel, H. and Cooper, C.L. (2000). *Destructive Conflict and Bullying at Work*, Manchester: School of Management, University of Manchester Institute of Science and Technology; Leymann (1996).

41 O'Moore, M. and Lynch, J. (2007). 'Leadership, Working Environment and Work-place Bullying. *International Journal of Organizational Theory and Behavior*, 10(1), 95–117.

42 Ashforth, B. (1994). 'Petty Tyranny in Organizations'. *Human Relations*, 4, 755–78.

boss abusive, but their behaviour can contribute to peer bullying, as aggressive behaviours are seen as the norm.[43]

ORGANIZATIONAL CHANGES

Given the relationships between stress and bullying, it should be no surprise to find that bullying has been linked to periods of organizational change.[44] One study found that 45.3 per cent of the victims were bullied following organizational change,[45] including budget cuts, changes in management and major restructuring.[46]

SECTOR DYNAMICS

Some things are beyond the manager's control, but you need to be aware of them and how they impact on your staff. For example, some industries have characteristics that make them more prone to bullying. It is particularly prevalent in the service sector, especially in health, public administration, education and financial services.[47] This may be because of the intangible nature of the work, which makes it difficult to measure performance. This lack of objective measures means that subjective judgements predominate.

Some researchers think that the increased emphasis on customer satisfaction is creating a situation where staff are increasingly bullied by customers. For example, one study revealed that 4.4 per cent of the health care professionals and teachers surveyed were bullied by their patients or students.[48] Leymann (1996) believes that nurses are particularly prone to bullying due to their heavy workload and the fact that they work under two supervisors.[49] Nurses must answer to both a doctor and a nurse supervisor – a situation that can lead to conflicting demands and uncertainty. It indicates a clear need for rules on the limits of the authority of each of their supervisors to allow greater role clarity, and a need to give workers greater control over their work.

Several human characteristics come to the surface during bullying. The most obvious is our need for control, and a number of studies reveal that

---

43 Hoel and Salin (2003).
44 Ibid.
45 Soares, A. (2002). *Bullying: When Work becomes Incident*, research report, Montreal: Université du Québec à Montréal.
46 Hoel and Cooper (2000).
47 Björkqvist, Osterman and Hjelt-Back (1994); Omari (2003).
48 Soares (2002).
49 Leymann (1996).

workers with limited control of their work are more likely to be victims of bullying. This suggests that if bullying is occurring in your workplace, it may be reduced by ensuring workers have sufficient control of their own work without excessive dependence on others. A second human trait is our tendency to social comparison. Many victims of bullying believe that envy is the core factor driving the behaviour of bullies.[50] A third feature is called the frustration-aggression hypothesis, which suggests that people's aggression levels rise when they suffer frustration.[51] If people are frustrated in their workplace, this gives rise to negative emotions which affect their interaction with those around them – hence the importance for managers of providing a workplace that is less likely to generate negative emotions.

Managers should be aware of a number of factors that contribute to dissatisfaction and frustration. You need to ensure that workers are not frustrated by organizational constraints or a lack of control over their own jobs.[52] Workers should have clear goals that reduce role conflict and ambiguity.[53] You also need to ensure that competition in the workplace does not get out of hand, and if necessary, you may need to change the reward/incentive system to reduce pressure from other staff.

A common finding of the research on bullying is that victims normally have less power than perpetrators. Because of this power imbalance, victims find it hard to defend themselves. Employees in socially exposed and visible situations are particularly vulnerable. This includes members of ethnic minorities and disabled employees with salaries subsidized by the government.[54] Women in many countries report higher victimization rates than men.[55] This suggests a connection between social and organizational power.

---

50 Einarsen, S. (2000). 'Harassment and Bullying at Work: A Review of the Scandinavian Approach'. *Aggression and Violent Behavior*, 5(4), 379–401.
51 Berkowitz, L. (1989). 'The Frustration-aggression Hypothesis: An Examination and Reformulation'. *Psychological Bulletin*, 106, 59–73.
52 Einarsen S., Raknes, B.I. and Matthiesen, S.B. (1994). 'Bullying and Harassment at Work and their Relationships to Work Environment Quality: An Exploratory Study'. *European Work and Organizational Psychologist*, 4(4), 381–401; Spector, P.E. (1997). 'The Role of Frustration in Anti-social Behavior at Work', in R.A. Giacalone and J. Greenberg (eds), *Anti-social Behavior in Organizations*, Thousand Oaks, CA: Sage; Vartia, M. (1996). 'The Sources of Bullying: Psychological Work Environment and Organizational Climate'. *European Journal of Work and Organizational Psychology*, 5(2), 203–14; Zapf, Knorz and Kulla (1996).
53 Vartia (1996); Einarsen, Raknes and Matthiesen (1994); Spector (1997).
54 Leymann, H. (1992). *Lönebidrag och Mobbad: En Svag Grupps Psykosociala Arbetsvillkor i Sverige* ('State Subsidies and the Bullied: A Vulnerable Group's Psycho-social Working Conditions in Sweden'), Stockholm: Arbetarskyddsstyrelsen; Hoel and Cooper (2000).
55 Aquino, K. and Bradfield, M. (2000). 'Perceived Victimization in the Workplace: The Role of Situational Factors and Victim Characteristics'. *Organization Science*, 11, 525–37; Cortina, L.M.,

Formal power differences are another source of such power imbalance, and in many cases, it is the boss who is the bully.[56] There are times in the employment relationship when the power balance reaches a point where employees become very exposed. This includes employees who lack job security. Fear of losing a job can make employees feel powerless in the face of an intimidating threatening supervisor. Consequently, bullying is more prevalent during periods of downsizing where job security is at risk.[57]

Workplaces characterized by poor planning, incompetent management and poor employee performance procedures also give rise to bullying. With little provision to measure performance, supervisors often resort to blaming staff for unmet goals. With no effective procedures to fall back on, the staff may feel intimidated and that they have to tolerate the abuse. The supervisor may feel that yelling and swearing at staff is one way of motivating them to perform better,[58] on the basis that 'Sometimes you use the carrot, and sometimes the stick.' This raises the possibility that you as a manager could have created a situation where your supervisors bully their staff because you have not organized work procedures sufficiently. This form of abuse can be reduced by introducing clearly defined goals and procedures for staff.

However, not all bullying by bosses is done to improve staff performance. In some cases, a supervisor for some reason perceives a staff member as a threat. The supervisor begins to behave in a heavy-handed way even though the employee may be perfectly competent. In other cases, bullying is stimulated by the human tendency for social comparison. Even though the supervisor is in a superior position, they too can exhibit these human weaknesses. In these cases, the bosses bully their subordinates because it gives them pleasure. It makes them feel superior.[59]

Magley, V.J., Williams, J.H. and Langhout, R.D. (2001). 'Incivility in the Workplace: Incidence and Impact'. *Journal of Occupational Health Psychology*, 6(1), 64–80; Hoel and Cooper (2000); Zapf, D., Knorz and Kulla (1996).

56 Cortina et al. (2001); Hoel and Cooper (2000); Knorz, C. and Zapf, D. (1996). 'Mobbing – eine extreme Form sozialer Stressoren am Arbeitsplatz' ('Mobbing – an Extreme Form of Social Stressor in the Workplace'). *Zeitschrift für Arbeits- und Organizationspsychologie*, 40(1), 12–21; O'Moore, M. (2000). *Summary Report on the National Survey on Workplace Bullying in Ireland*, Dublin: The Anti-Bullying Research Centre, Trinity College; Zapf, Knorz and Kulla (1996).

57 Sidle, S.D. (2009). 'Is Your Organization a Great Place for Bullies to Work?'. *Academy of Management Perspectives*, 23(4), 89–91.

58 Ibid.

59 Ibid.

Escalation Theories

Organizational factors may provide fertile soil for bullying, but this does not necessarily mean that it will occur. Workplace conditions are enabling factors that will give rise to bullying if an additional motivator or trigger exists. That trigger may be interpersonal or role conflict that, fuelled by frustration and negative emotion, becomes more serious. Some academics have noted how bullying can arise out of minor conflicts, and escalate. These escalation theories maintain that bullying may begin with a work-related conflict.[60] If the conflict is resolved early, the issue can end, but if not, it can escalate into harassment.[61] This places an onus on you as a manager to have intervention and conflict management strategies in place so that ill feeling does not escalate.

If the conflict is not resolved early, it can escalate, and one of the parties may find themselves in a disadvantaged position. They may find themselves stigmatized by their colleagues, at which point behaviour enters a new phase. The disadvantaged person is subjected to repeated and enduring aggressive acts. These take a number of forms, including humiliation and intimidation. It can include an attack on the person's self-image and self-esteem, giving rise to intense emotions. These emotions may include fear, suspicion, resentment, contempt and anger.[62] Because of their disadvantaged position, they may feel that they cannot defend themselves or escape. Having been stigmatized, victims find it harder to co-operate with others and complete their daily tasks. This poor performance further endorses the stigma and gives the appearance that they are 'a deserving target'.[63] The result is a bullying spiral.

Another researcher who observed how minor aggression can escalate into bullying is Kaj Björkqvist at the Abo Academy in Finland. According to Björkqvist, there are three phases in a typical harassment case.[64] In the first phase, the aggressive behaviour is indirect and discreet, which can make it difficult for a manager to identify. It may include spreading rumours or other

---

60 Leymann, H. (1990). 'Mobbing and Psychological Terror at Workplaces'. *Violence and Victims*, 5, 119–26.; Leymann, H. (1992). *Från Mobbning til Utslagning i Arbetslivet* ('From Bullying to Exclusion in the Labour Market'), Stockholm: Publica; Leymann, H. (1996). 'The Content and Development of Mobbing at Work'. *European Journal of Work and Organizational Psychology*, 5(2), 165–84.
61 Leymann (1992); Einarsen, Raknes and Matthiesen (1994).
62 Björkqvist, K. (1992). 'Trakassering Forekommer Bland Anstallda vid Abo Akademia' ('Harassment Occurs among Employees at Abo Academy'), *Meddelande fran Abo Akademi*, 9, 14–17.
63 Einarsen (2000).
64 Björkqvist (1992).

less overt forms of bullying, but behaviour escalates to a second phase, where more direct acts appear. This includes public humiliation. They are made fun of and feel increasingly isolated. In degrading the victim, the bully finds justification for what they say, which removes any sense of guilt. In these early phases, the victim is attacked only occasionally, but in the last phase, there is an increase in the frequency and harshness of attacks.[65] The victim is now subjected to both physical and psychological forms of violence. They may be accused of being psychologically ill, or personally threatened.

Although victims may have little ability to defend themselves, this does not mean they are totally passive. In fact, some victims have used strategies that helped to improve the situation. Zapf and Gross investigated people who were bullied to see whether those who coped successfully used different strategies to those who didn't cope.[66] They found that both successful and unsuccessful victims started with constructive conflict-solving. Often the first strategy was a passive 'wait and see' response. When this didn't work, the most common strategy was to talk to the bullies. However, this strategy was used more frequently by unsuccessful victims, which suggests it was not effective. Fighting back was another strategy used by unsuccessful victims, and once again it did not work. The unsuccessful ones tried a number of different strategies. Some informed their superiors, and even increased their loyalty to work, showing more effort.[67] When constructive strategies failed, victims turned to destructive strategies such as reducing commitment to the organization, and finally leaving.

A key difference between the successful and unsuccessful victims was their ability to recognize and avoid escalating behaviours. Given the human desire for reciprocity and justice, unsuccessful victims often fought back, but this only escalated the conflict. By contrast, the successful victims were less likely to fight back and resort to negative behaviour, although the rate of success was low. Studies reveal that only 6–12 per cent of victims were successful, which illustrates just how few options exist for victims. It also reinforces the need for you as a manager to introduce mechanisms that prevent bullying and enable early intervention to prevent escalation.[68]

---

65 Einarsen (2000).
66 Zapf, D. and Gross, C. (2001). 'Conflict Escalation and Coping with Workplace Bullying: A Replication and Extension'. *European Journal of Work and Organizational Psychology*, 10(4), 497–522.
67 Niedl, K. (1995), *Mobbing/Bullying am Arbeitsplatz* ('Mobbing/bullying in the Workplace'), Munich: Rainer Hampp Verlag. Neidl, K. (1996) 'Mobbing and Well-being: Economic and Personnel Development Implications'. *European Journal of Work and Organizational Psychology*, 5, 239–50.
68 Zapf and Gross (2001).

Interestingly, if the victim makes a legal complaint and supervisors are called in, the bullies perceive this as 'armament of the other party', which may lead to re-arming on their side. This can further escalate the conflict, and shows the importance of sensitivity and the need to understand the perspectives of both parties.[69]

Dealing with Bullying and Harassment

When you as a manager are called to deal with a claim of bullying, you will need to make a judgement about whether bullying has actually occurred, and if it has, how to deal with it. Some features of human nature could interfere with your judgement. First, if the victim has chosen a strategy of reduced commitment and absenteeism, you may feel inclined to think that criticism of this person is justified. This shows how bullying can be a vicious circle, as it leads to behavioural changes, which makes the target more vulnerable.[70]

You will have to come to terms with problems of attribution when attempting to determine the cause of the behaviour. In doing so, you need to avoid the fundamental attribution error, which is the human tendency to blame people for their own failings. This can lead us to believe that the victim is the cause of the trouble. Research from Scandinavia reveals that managers and other third parties 'seldom acknowledge the harm done to the victim as in fact bullying and harassment, but rather a no more than fair treatment of a difficult and neurotic person'.[71]

Other workplace features can distort attribution and may create a false impression of the victim. For example, in Chapter 5 we learned that some managers may treat their staff differently to others, creating a favoured in-group and an out-group. A victim of bullying from the boss is most likely to be in the out-group, but if the victim tells a colleague in the in-group, they are likely to be met with disbelief, as the boss has always treated the in-group members well. In such circumstances, the worker receives very little sympathy, and the colleague may believe that the victim is the cause of the problem. This raises the issue of care when interviewing staff about the issue.

---

69 Ibid.
70 Glasø, L., Matthiesen, S.B., Nielsen, M.B. and Einarsen, S. (2007). 'Do Targets of Workplace Bullying Portray a General Victim Personality Profile?'. *Scandinavian Journal of Psychology*, 48, 313–19.
71 Einarsen (2000), p. 392.

Human behaviour linked to cognitive dissonance can sometimes mean that innocent people receive a raw deal. You will recall that cognitive dissonance refers to when we hold two thoughts that are incompatible, so we often distort information to avoid that dissonance. This has relevance for bullying, harassment and other cases of victimization. For example, Janoff-Bulman proposed that people strive to maintain a belief (or schema) that the world is a benevolent and orderly place.[72] We also like to believe that we are good people. One can see that such a belief would make people happier, but what happens when we find evidence to the contrary?

Rather than changing their existing schema, this situation often sees people's thought processes distorting information so that innocent people might be perceived as being guilty. For example, if we believe the world is a just place, the Irish, who endured the Irish potato famine, must have done something to contribute to their plight. In believing the world is fair, we actually become less sensitive to people's problems and less accurate in our perceptions.[73] This has important implications for fairness in the workplace when workers have experienced an injustice. We may not be as sympathetic as the issue warrants, and we may attribute some of the blame to the worker.

Another cognitive distortion that can cause us to have less sympathy for the victim is the fundamental attribution error: the human tendency to attribute events to internal characteristics of the person involved. For example, if you don't have any problems with the so-called bully, you will tend to attribute the problem to the victim's personality.

On the other hand, just because a worker feels aggrieved does not mean that bullying has actually occurred. Bullying procedures and laws are not there to cover every bruised feeling or bad day at work.[74] You will need to determine whether the victim has actually been treated differently to other staff. However, if the answer is 'no', this does not necessary mean that you don't have a bullying case. Consider the example of Adare, the company described in Chapter 5 which had a culture of aggressive humour. Some staff at Adare may find the behaviour offensive even though it is the norm. You must

---

72 Janoff-Bulman, R. (1992). *Shattered Assumptions*, New York: Free Press.
73 Lerner, M.J. and Miller, D.T. (1977). 'Just World Research and the Attribution Process: Looking Back and Ahead'. *Psychological Bulletin*, 85, 1,030–51.
74 Yamada, D. (2003). 'Workplace Bullying and the Law: Towards a Transnational Consensus', in S. Einarsen, H. Hoel, D. Zapf and C.L. Cooper (eds), *Bullying and Emotional Abuse in the Workplace: International Perspectives in Research and Practice*, London and New York: Taylor & Francis, 399–411.

distinguish between negative behaviours that are tolerated and behaviours that are not tolerated. You must also identify whether victims find it difficult to defend themselves.

Behind all conflicts lie issues of differing perception. The perception of victims can be very different to the perception of perpetrators. In fact, perpetrators may be surprised that they are being accused of bullying. The difference in perception may reflect different schemas of social interaction. A person whose life experience tolerates a tougher approach to social interaction may come across as offensive to someone with a schema of sensitivity.

It may be unfair to label someone as a 'bully' if they are simply continuing the social practices they have been brought up with. However, such people can be told of the effect their behaviour is having. If they are made aware of this without applying negative labels, it will not arouse defensive reactions and is more likely to lead to behavioural change, but of course, this depends on the level of infringement.

All staff members do not have the same level of resilience, and in some cases, the manager may be tempted to tell the worker to toughen up, but under most countries' laws, they cannot do this. You must take into account the victim's perception of the incident, knowing full well the subjective nature of both the victim's and the perpetrator's perceptions.

Academics stress the difference between *subjective harassment* and *objective harassment*.[75] Managers are interested in subjective harassment as it reveals a sense of real pain suffered by the target – something managers would like to reduce. Subjective harassment also informs management about how the victim perceives their interaction with others at work.[76] However, subjective harassment is not evidence that harassment or bullying has occurred.

Objective harassment is 'a situation where actual external evidence of harassment is found'.[77] To find evidence of objective harassment, you will need to explore any evidence given by the victim and perpetrator. This may include statements from co-workers, employers or independent observers. The situation must be appraised to identify anything that could be considered threatening or offensive.

---

75 Einarsen (2000), p. 397.
76 Niedl (2005).
77 Einarsen (2000), p. 397.

If an aggressive culture exists or if a supervisor finds that bullying is a good way to control staff, it is unlikely to stop without effective organizational action.[78] The way an organization responds to bullying is important in maintaining staff loyalty. Perceived organizational support has a significant impact on whether bullied staff intend to leave.[79] Managers need to demonstrate that the organization cares for their welfare. You should inform your staff that the organization will not tolerate such behaviour. This includes developing formal policies and procedures that illustrate that the organization takes the matter seriously. A policy on bullying will include:

1.   issuing a statement of general principles that the organization is committed to – this will most likely include a statement that bullying will not be tolerated, a recognition that staff must be treated with dignity and respect, and a statement that all staff are expected to comply with the policy or face disciplinary action;

2.   drawing up a definition of bullying and acts that constitute bullying;

3.   making a Contact Manager available, independent from existing staff and management, which will give staff the option of gaining independent advice; the contact manager should not be involved in any complaints procedure as this means they will gain extra work if they encourage a formal complaint; they must be objective;

4.   setting up complaints procedures which outline the steps the organization will take if a complaint is received.[80]

There are a number of ways a complaint can be dealt with. An effective strategy is problem-solving or conciliation, in which the victim and perpetrator discuss the problem with the goal of resolving it. However, this is only likely to be a useful option in the early stages when emotions are not aroused. Few victims feel that they can directly confront their abusers.

---

78 Sidle (2009).
79 Djurkovic, N., McCormack, D. and Casimir, G. (2008). 'Workplace Bullying and Intention to Leave: The Moderating Effect of Perceived Organizational Support'. *Human Resource Management Journal*, 18(4), 405–22.
80 Adapted from Richards, J. and Daley, H. (2003). 'Bullying Policy: Development, Implementation and Monitoring', in S. Einarsen, H. Hoel, D. Zapf and C. Cooper (eds), *Bullying and Emotional Abuse in the Workplace: International Perspectives in Research and Practice*, London: Taylor & Francis.

Mediation is an option in which a third party facilitates the meeting and helps to remove any sense of intimidation the victim may feel. But once again, mediation assumes that the parties are equally capable of negotiating – an assumption that is unlikely in bullying cases. Furthermore, mediation seeks to resolve the issue to ensure that it doesn't happen in the future. It does not address or punish past actions, and may leave the victim with a sense that justice has not been served.[81]

Arbitration is where a third party settles the dispute, and this is seen as an appropriate way to deal with a case if the conflict has reached a stage where mediation will not work. Arbitration is appropriate where hostility is serious, but there is still some possibility to find agreement. If the level of aggression is worse than this, it may be necessary to appoint someone as a peace-keeper to ensure the conflict does not escalate any further.

When deciding which approach to adopt, you must have a good sense of the history and state of the relationship so that you can apply the appropriate procedure. If you apply the wrong method, your procedures may fail.[82]

The goal of the procedures should be to modify the harasser's behaviour, protect the target and deter other organizational members from engaging in similar conduct.[83] If a case of bullying is upheld, it may be necessary to transfer or dismiss the bully, depending on its seriousness. Alternatively, in order to modify future behaviour, it may be appropriate to provide counselling and training. The bully must be made aware what aspects of their behaviour cause offence. It may also be necessary to offer counselling to the victim, who may have suffered significant psychological harm.

In some cases, separating the two parties is a logical solution, transferring one of them to another department. However, it is often easier to move the victim, especially if the bully is the boss. The victim may feel that is unfair that they have to leave and the perpetrator is allowed to stay, especially if their new job is not as satisfying.[84]

Sheehan and Jordan (2003) suggest that managers should draw on concepts from the learning organization when dealing with bullying and harassment

---

81 Keashly and Nowell (2003).
82 Ibid.
83 Salin, D. (2009). 'Organizational Responses to Workplace Harassment: An Exploratory Study. *Personnel Review*, 38(1), 26–44.
84 Zapf and Gross (2001).

cases.[85] They argue that such cases can be reduced if organizations and their staff continuously improve their skills and abilities. This includes people becoming more attuned to their emotions and those of others. In the case of bullies, this may mean acknowledging inappropriate behaviour and apologizing. People are not always aware of their actions or their consequences. They should take the opportunity to learn how to regulate their emotions to improve relationships with others in the workplace.

An approach based on learning may also require a change in mental models about how management in the workplace is conducted and what is considered appropriate behaviour. It requires the adoption of a model in which bullying is not tolerated. The goal is not to abolish conflict in the workplace, as this will never be achieved, but to recognize that conflict should be constructive, not dysfunctional. Conflict should focus on problems and issues, not individuals. As football players say: 'Play the ball, not the man.'

The learning organization approach is consistent with the human model presented in this book, which argues that humans have limited capabilities and make mistakes. We also have limited self-perception, so we need to maximize self-learning opportunities when we goof. This is not to say that offenders should escape reprimand (especially repeat offenders). Bullies should be made to consider the consequences of their actions, as well led to understand the attitudes and emotions that lead them to bully in the first place. They should also be given self-management strategies to help prevent them lapsing back into negative behaviours.

Sheehan and Jordan argue that a learning approach is more likely to ameliorate bullying and improve workplace relations. While this provides an optimistic view of a destructive activity, we must not forget that bullying is exactly that – a destructive activity with very real costs to the organization and staff. Instead of spending time and resources dealing with complaints procedures, managers would be better to use their time preventing these issues arising in the first place. As a manager, you can reduce the amount of time you spend on these cases if you focus on improving the overall work environment to avoid the build-up of individual stress, remove destructive imbalances of power and role uncertainty, and ensure that boundaries of offensive behaviour are

---

85 Sheehan, M.J. and Jordan, P.J. (2003). 'Bullying, Emotions and the Learning Organization', in S. Einarsen, H. Hoel, D. Zapf and C.L. Cooper (eds), *Bullying and Emotional Abuse in the Workplace: International Perspectives in Research and Practice*, London and New York: Taylor & Francis, 259–69.

understood and maintained. It is your job to ensure that relationships between staff contribute to productivity, rather than reducing personal well-being.

7

Sex

I had just had dinner and was settling in for a quiet night in front of the TV, when the phone rang. It was Nicki, the wife of my head foreman. She asked me if I knew what was going on.

I didn't know that anything was going on, so she told me. Her husband was having an affair with my chief designer. Nicki asked me what I was going to do about it.

I didn't know if I could do anything about it. We had no company policies on dating or adultery, and I couldn't sack them for what they did outside of work. But it was a problem. These were two of my three most important staff. I couldn't afford to lose either of them, and if things got out of hand, I was bound to lose at least one.

In the end, I bluffed. I called the two in to my office and said if they didn't put an end to it, I would have to let one of them go.

Fortunately, the 'romance' had not progressed very far, and they stopped it then and there.

Sex is one of our most important core motives. Our motivation to be engaged in sex is essential for the existence of the human species, so it can only be expected that sexual behaviours may flow in to the workplace. Traditionally, workplace romances were seen as inappropriate, but in recent years they have become an increasingly common part of work life.[1] This is particularly prevalent among younger employees, and a number of factors have contributed to this. They include a change in traditional gender roles, the presence of more women in the workforce, and the fact that the long time spent together at work creates an excellent opportunity for people to get to know one another.[2]

---

1   Cole, N. (2009). 'Workplace Romance: A Justice Analysis'. *Journal of Business Psychology*, 24, 363–72.
2   Powers, D.M. (1998). *The Office Romance: Playing With Fire without Getting Burned*. New York: AMACOM.

Workplace romances are not without their problems. First, those in romances must recognize that public displays of affection may not be appreciated by other staff. They need to maintain professional interaction with each other, despite their underlying feelings.[3] A concern among other staff may be that the parties in the romance receive preferential treatment, particularly if the relationship is between a supervisor and a subordinate. This can create resentment.[4] Perhaps the greatest concern arises when the relationship ends, particularly if one of the parties wants the relationship to continue. This can create patterns of distrust, with people taking sides and reputations being destroyed.[5] Finally, there is the fear of a sexual harassment claim, as attorney Alan Kopit notes: 'Dating a co-worker can start out as a consensual relationship, until the relationship ends. One person may get upset and claim they were forced into the relationship, or that they didn't get a raise or a promotion because of a breakup.'[6]

Workers in the highest echelons of organizations have been caught out by their biological drive. For example, in 2007, the President of the American Red Cross lost his job because he had a relationship with a subordinate. Women are not immune. In 2002, Suzy Wetlaufer, Editor-in-Chief at *Harvard Business Review*, was forced to resign after having a workplace dalliance. She was expected to conduct an interview with Jack Welch, the CEO of General Electric, but ended up having an affair with him.[7] Homosexual lovers have also been caught up in such scandals. In 2007, the Chief Executive of British Petroleum, Lord John Brown, resigned when revelations about his former partner were raised in the press. On leaving his job, he stated: 'For the past 41 years of my career at BP, I have kept my private life separate from my business life. I have always regarded my sexuality as a personal matter, to be kept private.'[8]

Increasingly, workers are in agreement with Lord Brown. Many feel that an individual's romance is none of the company's business. A number of surveys have been conducted which reveal an acceptance of workplace romances. Two studies conducted in 2005 and 2006 found that only 4–6 per cent of people

3   Ibid.
4   Pearce, J. (2010). 'What Execs Don't Get About Office Romance'. *MIT Sloan Management Review*, 51(3), 39–40.
5   Ibid.
6   Kopit, A. (2004). 'Research Reveals Rise in Interoffice Romance', http://research.lawyers.com/ Research-Reveals-Rise-in-Interoffice-Romance.html, accessed 20 July 2013.
7   Boyd, C. (2010). 'The Debate over the Prohibition of Romance in the Workplace'. *Journal of Business Ethics*, 97(2), 325–38.
8   Mufson, S. (2007). 'BP Chief Resigns Abruptly over Relationship Furor', *Washington Post*, 2 May.

believed that a workplace romance 'is or should not be permitted'. A similarly small number disapproved of an employee dating a vendor.[9] For example, a 2005 study conducted by the Society for Human Resource Management and the *Wall Street Journal* found that 40 per cent of employees had participated in a workplace romance.[10] Similar results were found in a 2009 study.[11] An earlier study reported that 71 per cent of respondents had dated someone at work and 50 per cent of managers had dated a subordinate.[12]

It would seem that one overwhelming reason why these relationships are approved of is the importance they have in people's lives. Many of the relationships lead to marriage. Three in ten people met their spouses at work, according to one survey.[13] As John Pearce of Villanova University states: 'By permitting office romances, companies provide what many employees see as a prime benefit of employment with the company – an opportunity to enrich their social lives.'[14]

One of the problems for you as a manager is the broad range of views you will have to contend with on the subject. All of your workers will have their own schema. For example, one survey showed that 42 per cent of workers thought that if their supervisor complimented their body or physique, it was welcome flirting. However, 36 per cent thought it was uncomfortable attention. The difference has much to do with gender. Men are much more likely to be comfortable with flirting, 61 per cent welcoming compliments from a female supervisor. By contrast only 20 per cent of women welcomed compliments from a male supervisor.[15]

Of course, much will depend on the relationship and the people involved, but it is often the case that what one person enjoys, another person will perceive as a threat. Ideally, as a manager, you should strive to protect all your workers, but some workers hold views that suggest they have no idea about normal

9   Gurchiek, K. (2006). 'Most Organizations Lack Policy on Office Romance', 9 February, http://www.globalethics.org/newsline/2006/02/13/most-organizations-lack-policy-on-office-romance/, accessed 20 July 2013.
10 Parks, M. (2006). *Workplace Romance: Poll findings*, Alexandria, VA: Society for Human Resource Management.
11 CareerBuilder.com (2009). 'Forty Percent of Workers Have Dated a Co-worker, Finds Annual CareerBuilder.com Valentine's Day Survey', http://www.careerbuilder.co.uk/share/about us/pressreleasesdetail.aspx?sd=2%2F10%2F2009&id=pr481&ed=12%2F31%2F2009, accessed 20 July 2013.
12 Solomon, C.M. (1998). 'The Truth of Workplace Romance'. *Workforce*, 77(7), 42–50.
13 CareerBuilder.com (2009).
14 Pearce (2010).
15 Kopit (2004).

interaction. But what is normal interaction? You will feel that your views are normal, and tend to support workers who have the same schema as you.

While there is a growing belief that workplace romances should be tolerated, it is wise for employers to create suitable policies given the problems that can occur. However, recent research reveals that over 70 per cent of organizations do not have workplace romance policies.[16] In theory, this gives employees great freedom, but it can also leave them open to arbitrary decisions. Most human resource managers do not believe that, for example, relationships between staff and supervisors are advisable, but neither do they believe restrictions are desirable. They keep an eye on relationships that they are aware of, and do not intervene unless the relationship violates company policies or leads to workplace dysfunction.[17]

Some companies require employees to report relationships to their supervisors.[18] One option proposed to manage workplace relationships and prevent harassment claims is to get participants to sign a consensual relationship agreement.[19] When the workers sign the agreement, they confirm that the relationship is consensual, that they will not engage in favouritism, and that neither will take any legal action against the employer or each other if the relationship founders.[20] The agreement may also specify appropriate behaviours at work, particularly if the relationship comes to an end.

Some employers may have rules that forbid workers from dating clients or employees of competing companies. Some organizations have bans on workplace relations that are driven by specific moral codes. These include religion-based schools. Such groups have an unlikely ally in radical feminists, who oppose workplace romance in order to protect women from unwelcome attention and the possibility of harassment.[21] However, a more recent wave of feminists have opposed this view and its puritanical oppressions. For example, Wendy McElroy notes:

> *somewhere along the line the rebellious joy has drained out of the feminist movement. Instead of celebrating the pleasures of sex, women are now*

16 Parks (2006).
17 Ibid.
18 Kiser, S.B., Tyne, C., Ford, M. and Moore, E. (2006). 'Coffee, Tea or Me? Romance and Sexual Harassment in the Workplace'. *Southern Business Review*, 31(2), 35–49.
19 Pierce, C.A. and Aguinis, H. (2001). 'A Framework for Investigating the Link between Workplace Romance and Sexual Harassment'. *Group & Organization Management*, 26(2), 206–29.
20 Boyd (2010).
21 Ibid.

*barraged only by its perils: rape, domestic violence, harassment. ...
Now women are portrayed as victims of oppression. Gone is the
emphasis on independence and spunk. ... A certain go-to-hell spirit
has been replaced by a life-is-hell attitude, and with it a strange new
puritanism has gripped the feminist movement.*[22]

*The issue of sexual harassment has prompted a politically correct
inquisition, with the goal of rooting out and punishing men who express
attitudes deemed to be improper towards women.*[23]

Pierce and Aguinis (2009) state that there are 10 million new workplace romances
in the United States each year.[24] This compares to an average of 14,200 sexual
harassment claims per year, suggesting that for every case of harassment, there
are 704 romances. Given that many harassment claims are not a result of failed
romances, the true ratio may be as low as 1 in 5,000. Even accepting that many
harassment cases are not reported, these figures suggest that harassment is not
a good reason to stop workers from finding romance.

Given that the majority of workplace romances end up in marriage or long-
term partnerships, McElroy's position would appear to be the strongest. Denying
workers the opportunity for romance also denies them an opportunity to pursue a
basic human need. A survey conducted by the American Management Association
revealed that 44 per cent of workplace romances led to marriage, while another
23 per cent led to a long-term relationship.[25] Further research reveals that couples
working in the same workplace have a 50 per cent lower rate of divorce.[26] Many
researchers have come to the conclusion that the workplace is the best place to
meet your future life partner.[27] Work-based romances develop gradually over
months and years, allowing people to get to know one another.[28] It may be one of
the aspects where work makes a significant contribution to our happiness.

---

22 McElroy, W. (1996). *Sexual Correctness: The Gender Feminist Attack on Women*, Jefferson, NC:
    McFarland, p. 6.

23 Ibid., p. 62.

24 Pierce, C.A. and Aguinis, H. (2009). 'Moving Beyond a Legal-centric Approach to Managing
    Workplace Romances: Organizationally Sensible Recommendations for HR Leaders'. *Human
    Resource Management*, 48(3), 447–64.

25 AMA (American Management Association) (2003). '44% of Office Romances Led to Marriage,
    AMA Survey Shows', press release, 10 February, http://www.amanet.org/press/amanews/
    workplace_dating.htm, accessed 8 February 2007.

26 Aberg, Y. (2004). *Is Divorce Contagious? The Marital Status of Co-workers and the Risk of Divorce*,
    working paper, Oxford: Nuffield College.

27 Boyd (2010).

28 Losee, S. and Olen, H. (2007). *Office Mate: The Employee Handbook for Finding – and Managing –
    Romance on the Job*, Avon, MA: Adams Media.

Flirting

The human mating process conventionally begins with flirting. This is where the first indications of interest are exchanged. However, flirting can be an exceptionally confusing form of communication. Some academics believe that flirting is intentionally ambiguous.[29] In fact, academic definitions of flirting stress this ambiguity. For example, Henningsen, Braz and Davies (2008) define flirting as 'ambiguous goal-motivated behaviours that can be, but are not restricted to being, interpreted as sexually motivated'.[30]

When someone flirts with us, the behaviour suggests that they are sexually interested in us, but the ambiguous nature means we cannot confirm this is actually the case. People may flirt for a number of reasons. Individuals may flirt to promote sexual contact or to advance a relationship, but they may also do it simply because they find it enjoyable and it makes them feel good. Henningsen (2004) identified six reasons why people choose to flirt.[31] Only three of these are linked to mating. They include a sexual motivation, a relational motivation and an 'exploring' motivation, in which people are exploring the potential for a romantic relationship. However, three of the motives have nothing to do with mating. People flirt to boost their self-esteem (esteem motivation), to encourage others to do things for them (instrumental motivation) or just to have fun (fun motivation).

Research suggests that much flirting in the workplace and at university is motivated simply by the desire to have fun.[32] In such cases, it is a momentary distraction with no long-term implications for sex or relationships. People flirt because they enjoy it. Feelings of self-esteem and belonging may lie beneath that enjoyment.

Downey and Vitulli found that individuals may flirt to build their self-esteem.[33] People feel flattered when others give them attention, and this encourages them to flirt. They end up feeling attractive, desirable and

---

29 Grammer, K., Kruck, K., Juette, A. and Fink, B. (2000). 'Non-verbal Behavior as Courtship Signals: The Role of Control and Choice in Selecting Partners'. *Evolution and Human Behavior*, 21(6), 371–90; Haselton and Buss (2000).

30 Henningsen, D.D., Braz, M. and Davies, E. (2008). 'Why Do We Flirt? Flirting Motivations and Sex Differences in Working and Social Contexts'. *Journal of Business Communication*, 45(4), 483–502.

31 Henningsen, D.D. (2004). 'Flirting with Meaning: An Examination of Miscommunication in Flirting Interactions'. *Sex Roles*, 50(7–8), 481–9.

32 Henningsen, Braz and Davies (2008).

33 Downey, J.L. and Vitulli, W.F. (1987). 'Self-report Measures of Behavioral Attributions Related to Interpersonal Flirtation Situations'. *Psychological Reports*, 61, 899–904.

interesting. In fact, some people choose jobs for this reason. Loe (1996) studied a restaurant chain where female staff, as part of their job, wore revealing uniforms and flirted with their primarily male clientele.[34] Loe found that some women take these jobs because the appreciation they receive from males boosts their self-esteem and affirms their femininity.

Perhaps the least desirable motive is instrumental flirting, in which people flirt to try to get something. Research has revealed that women do sometimes flirt for instrumental purposes.[35] In some cases, such flirting is actually encouraged at work. For example, it is not uncommon for employers in the hospitality industry to encourage their wait staff to flirt with customers in order to increase spending or gain repeated custom.[36] Some managers consider it part of the job.

Flirting for rewards has also been reported at universities. In one study, Rowland, Crisler and Cox (1982) found that it was a commonly held belief that flirting with their instructors would assist their grades.[37] Both male and female students held this view. Nearly three quarters believed that a female student flirting with a male supervisor would receive a higher grade.

Flirting can be very subtle, but researchers have been able to identify a number of behaviours used, some of which are listed in Table 7.1. Many of them have the effect of saying, 'Look at my body.'[38]

When it comes to flirting, there are large differences between men and women, and there may be an evolutionary explanation. If women make a bad choice in the mating process, they can be left with a significantly higher cost compared to males. To ensure they attract a good partner, women 'need to develop a large repertoire of flirting behaviours'.[39] They may even use flirting as a way of maintaining a man's interest while assessing another potential partner.

---

34 Loe, K. (1996). 'Working for Men: At the Intersection of Power, Gender, and Sexuality'. *Sociological Inquiry*, 66, 399–421.
35 Yelvington, K.A. (1996). 'Flirting in the Factory'. *Journal of the Royal Anthropological Institute*, 2, 313–33.
36 Gilbert, D., Guerrier, Y. and Guy, J. (1998). 'Sexual Harassment Issues in the Hospitality Industry'. *International Journal of Contemporary Hospitality Management*, 10, 48–53.
37 Rowland, D.L., Crisler, L.J. and Cox, D.J. (1982). 'Flirting between College Students and Faculty'. *Journal of Sex Research*, 18, 346–59.
38 Goffmann, E. (1979). *Gender Advertisements*, London: Macmillan.
39 Trost, M.R. and Alberts, J.K. (1998). 'An Evolutionary View on Understanding Sex Effects in Communicating Attraction', in D.J. Canary and K. Dindia (eds), *Sex Differences and Similarities in Communication: Critical Essays and Empirical Investigations of Sex and Gender in Interaction*, Mahwah, NJ: Erlbaum, pp. 233–55.

Table 7.1   Forms of flirting

Primp	Adjusting one's clothes without a visible need to do so
Head toss	The head moves down, followed by a fast circular upward movement, then the head slowly returns to the original position
Hair flip	Similar movement to *head toss*, except that the hands are used to throw the hair back
Neck presentation	A sideward *head tilt*, suggesting submission or avoidance of 'staring eyes' when eye contact occurs
Breast presentation	Both shoulders are moved back simultaneously
Palm	Both palms are presented upwards
Head down	The head and gaze is lowered (alleged to be a sign of submission in courtship)
Shrug	The shoulders are repeatedly moved up and down
Coy smile	A smile followed by a turning away and lowering of the head
Legs open	When sitting
Look through	Looking at the target, but not fixating on them, then looking away immediately
Short glance	Directed at the partner for less than three seconds
Illustrator	Uses illustrating hand movements when speaking
Arms flex	One or both arms are flexed at the elbow and held in front of the body
Smile	
Laugh	

Source: Adapted from K. Grammer, K. Kruck, A. Juette and B. Fink (2000). 'Non-verbal Behavior as Courtship Signals: The Role of Control and Choice in Selecting Partners'. *Evolution and Human Behavior*, 21(6), 371–90.

Research suggests that females are more interested in developing the art of flirting. For example, Moore (1995) found that adolescent girls actually practised flirting.[40] In mixed-sex situations, the girls displayed an array of flirting behaviours which Moore believed was being done to refine their expertise. However, flirting is not the only occasion when women excel when using and understanding body language. Even as children, females exhibit greater use and understanding of non-verbal behaviour than males.[41] Women generally have better-developed expertise in the use of non-verbal behaviour for self-presentational purposes. Their 'body movements are more involved and more expressive'.[42]

40 Moore, M.M. (1995). 'Courtship Signaling and Adolescents: Girls Just Wanna Have Fun?'. *Journal of Sex Research*, 32(4), 319–28.
41 Argyle, M. (1988). *Bodily Communication*, London: Methuen; Henley, N. and LaFrance, M. (1984). 'Gender as Culture: Difference and Dominance in Non-verbal Behaviour', in A. Wolfgang (ed.), *Non-verbal Behaviour. Perspectives, Applications, Intercultural Insights*, Lewiston, NY: Hogrefe, pp. 351–72.
42 DePaulo, B.M. (1992). 'Non-verbal Behavior and Self-presentation'. *Psychological Bulletin*, 111, 203–243, pp. 222–3.

The consequence is that there are huge differences between men's and women's abilities to recognize what is happening during flirting, with women being far more attuned. When asked, women can describe how they and others flirt to pick up men with high levels of accuracy. Men, in contrast, seem to have no idea what is happening.[43] When men were asked, a common response was, 'I just know it works out.'[44] This suggests that women are actually controlling the courtship/flirting process, and the evidence suggests that women do manipulate men in a non-obvious way.[45] Grammer et al. (2000) describe how this is done: 'If a woman is interested in a man, female rhythmic body movements create "hidden" and highly complex patterns in synchrony with the male body movements. The man perceives changes in her interest but is not able to ascertain their source.'[46]

On the basis of their research, Grammer et al. suggest that when meeting a potential mate, women may try to 'control' the man's behaviour. They will deliberately send out ambiguous signals to hide their own intentions while trying to determine the man's intentions. To do this, they will send out signals of interest followed by signals of disinterest. They use non-verbal behaviour to force men to reveal their hand. Men confronted with this erratic behaviour will be more inclined to express their interest verbally and directly, knowing full well that other men may be interested if they do not act. This description suggests that men are accustomed to acting even though the feedback they receive from women is ambiguous and sometimes negative.

The problem when considering flirting in sexual harassment cases is its intangible nature. An accused male may not be able to identify specific behaviours, and even if he does, he will sound particularly weak if he claims the woman engaged in 'neck presentation'. However, such behaviours do prompt action in men. To make matters worse, some women may not be conscious of the fact that they are doing it. I regularly ask the girls in my class whether they have a friend who flirts without knowing it. They invariably answer 'yes'. I then ask them whether the girl they identified has a friend who also flirts without knowing it. In other words, they may at times be flirting but not aware

43 Perper, T. and Fox, V.S. (1980). 'Flirtation and Pickup Pattern in Bars', paper presented at the Eastern Conference on Reproductive Behavior, New York.
44 Kirkendall, L. (1961). *Premarital Intercourse and Interpersonal Relationships*, New York: Julian Press.
45 Grammer, K., Kruck, K. and Magnusson, M. (1998). 'The Courtship Dance: Patterns of Non-verbal Synchronization in Opposite Sex Encounters'. *Journal of Non-verbal Behavior*, 22(1), 3–29.
46 Grammer et al. (2000), p. 373.

they are doing so (I then have to remind the guys in the class that they have similar gaps in self-knowing).

Sexual Harassment

Rates of reported harassment vary from 5 per cent for Norwegian women to 36 per cent for women in the United States.[47] Regardless of the rates, it is your job as a manager to ensure that your employees are not working in a hostile environment. This means that you must protect your workers from all forms of harassment. Sexual harassment is normally a case where women perceive they are victims of inappropriate male action, but it can be the other way around. It can also include homosexual or lesbian activity.

Gender harassment can include a wide range of behaviours, including offensive remarks, jokes and insults. Table 7.2 categorizes seven different types of behaviours that can be interpreted as sexual harassment.[48] The first category refers to behaviours in which derogatory attitudes are espoused against women (or men) in general. An example of this would be the poster at Adare described in Chapter 5 in which a man stood over a beaten woman. While this behaviour is directed at all women, the second category is derogatory of an individual person because of their gender. It may include criticism of a person's ability, followed by saying it is because they are a woman or gay/lesbian. The third category is unwanted dating pressure. Merely asking someone out is not considered harassment, as this is considered normal activity. However, if requests for a date continue after they have been rejected, it can be interpreted as harassment. The fourth category goes beyond asking for a date, referring to requests for sexual encounters. The fifth category is physical sexual contact, and refers to behaviours where physical contact has actually occurred, for example kissing the colleague. However, some physical contact is not sexually motivated. This is physical non-sexual contact, an example of which is giving someone a congratulatory hug. None of these first six categories include coercion, but that changes with the last category. These are requests for sexual encounters that are backed up with threats, or are expected in return for promotion or job placement.

---

47 Einarsen, S. (2000). 'Harassment and Bullying at Work: A Review of the Scandinavian Approach'. *Aggression and Violent Behavior*, 5(4), 379–401.
48 Rotundo, M., Nguyen, D.H. and Sackett, P.R. (2001). 'A Meta-analytic Review of Gender Differences in Perceptions of Sexual Harassment'. *Journal of Applied Psychology*, 86(5), 914–22.

Table 7.2   Behavioural categories of sexual harassment

Category	Description	Behavioural examples
Derogatory attitudes – impersonal	Behaviours that reflect derogatory attitudes about men or women in general	Obscene gestures not directed at target Sex-stereotyped jokes
Derogatory attitudes– personal	Behaviours that are directed at the target that reflect derogatory attitudes about the target's gender	Obscene phone calls Belittling the target's competence
Unwanted dating pressure	Persistent requests for dates after the target has refused	Repeated requests for a date
Sexual propositions	Explicit requests for sexual encounters	Proposition for an affair
Physical sexual contact	Behaviour in which the harasser makes physical sexual contact with the target	Embracing or kissing the target
Physical non-sexual contact	Behaviour in which the harasser makes physical non-sexual contact with the target	Congratulatory hug
Sexual coercion	Requests for sexual encounters or forced encounters that are made a condition of employment or promotion	Threaten punishment unless sexual favours given Sexual bribery

Source: Data from M. Rotundo, D.H. Nguyen and P.R. Sackett (2001). 'A Meta-analytic Review of Gender Differences in Perceptions of Sexual Harassment'. *Journal of Applied Psychology*, 86(5), 914–22.

In reading about these categories, you may question whether they actually constitute harassment. For example, many people will not believe that physical non-sexual contact constitutes sexual harassment. Some of these forms of harassment have very little to do with our motive for sex, and seem more closely connected to our tendency for social comparison and the desire for superior status. Some of these activities more properly belong in Chapter 5, in which we discussed boundaries of humour. Different forms of sexual harassment can be driven by different motives.[49] Regardless of the motive, certain types of harassment are against the law and need to be addressed.

Given that harassing is a very bad way to woo a woman, we can expect that harassment is probably driven by motives other than sex. Many forms of harassment can be linked to the motives of control and self-esteem (power), and would appear to be variations of bullying. Research has found that harassment can be linked with power, and as with bullying, the victims are most likely to be in positions of vulnerability (younger, of single marital status and with lower

---

49 Fitzgerald, L.F. and Shullman, S.L. (1993). 'Sexual Harassment: A Research Analysis and Agenda for the 1990s'. *Journal of Vocational Behavior*, 42(1), 5–27.

levels of education).[50] It is more likely to occur in male-dominated industries and in organizations that tolerate sexual harassment.[51]

In the rest of this chapter, we will focus on how differences in human nature can influence this topic. However, it must be stressed at the outset that the following discussion only applies to certain types of sex-based conflict. The goal of this chapter is to gain a greater understanding of human nature and gender differences so that we can reduce and deal more effectively with cases of sexual harassment.

Differences between the Sexes

An important theory that suggests there are gender differences in how we view mating is Robert Trivers's (1972) Theory of Parental Investment.[52] This theory looks at why we mate in the first place, and how it might affect mating behaviour. Given that the woman must carry the child and perform more nurturing functions, she is likely to be choosy when selecting a mate. In contrast, the man has less need to be choosy, and is more concerned with finding opportunities to mate. This leaves us with two different approaches to sexual interaction: choosy females, and males who operate with less caution.

How important are these different views?' One theory suggests that the difference between the genders may be great, and this has implications for sexual harassment in the workplace. In Chapter 2, we noted that humans have many cognitive biases. Error Management Theory looks at how these biases may have developed as humans evolved.[53] This theory notes that when faced with uncertainty, humans will make errors. For example, if a man is interested in a woman but is uncertain whether she is interested, he can hit on her, in which case he may get lucky or he may be rejected. Alternatively, he can choose not to hit on her, and be guaranteed to miss out completely. In evolutionary terms, the best error for the man to make is the first one, as this has the greatest

---

50 Hesson-McInnis, M. and Fitzgerald, L.F. (1992). 'Predicting the Outcomes of Sexual Harassment A Preliminary Test', paper presented to the 2nd Annual AOA/NIOSH Conference on Stress and the Workplace, Washington DC, November; Tangri, S.S., Burt, M.R. and Johnson, L.B. (1982). 'Sexual Harassment at Work: Three Explanatory Models'. *Journal of Social Issues*, 38, 33–54.
51 Fitzgerald and Shullman (1993).
52 Trivers, R.L. (1972). 'Parental Investment and Sexual Selection', in B. Campbell (ed.) *Sexual Selection and the Descent of Man, 1871–1971*, Chicago, IL: Aldine, pp. 136–79.
53 Haselton M.G. and Buss, D.M. (2000). 'Error Management Theory: A New Perspective on Biases in Cross-sex Mind Reading'. *Journal of Personality and Social Psychology*, 78(1), 81–91.

chance of leading to the reproduction of his genes. It is the best option as there is less chance of failure.

Error Management Theory suggests that men have a natural cognitive bias towards interpreting interaction with women as an opportunity whereas in many instances that opportunity does not exist. A large number of experiments by psychologists suggest that men actually possess this bias. Studies that compare men's perceptions of women's sexual intent with women's perceptions reveal that men consistently over-judge the sexual intentions of women.[54] Sadly for men, when psychologists studied women's interpretations of men's behaviour, they found little evidence of bias.[55] This is not to say that women do not make mistakes, but it appears that men are naturally wired to make an error of optimism.

In one study, women and men were asked whether a member of the opposite sex had ever misinterpreted their friendly behaviour as sexual interest. The results found that 72 per cent of women and 60 per cent of men had experienced a member of the opposite sex overestimating their sexual interest.[56] It would seem that the majority of both sexes make mistakes, but a higher proportion of men do. Of course, this could just mean that men are worse at interpreting signals, or alternatively, that women's signals are more ambiguous and harder to interpret.

If it is a case of difficulty in reading messages, we would expect men to not only make mistakes in overestimating women's interest, but to also make mistakes in under-interpreting it. To see whether this was the case, Haselton (2003) asked men and women about the number of times they had their messages over-interpreted and under-interpreted, the latter being a time when they had sent messages that they were interested in someone but that person failed to read them correctly.[57] The results supported the finding that men have a tendency to overestimate women's interest.

This finding has important implications for understanding sexual harassment studies. An example of this can be seen at a Safeway supermarket

---

54 Haselton, M.G. (2003). 'The Sexual Over-perception Bias: Evidence of a Systematic Bias in Men from a Survey of Naturally Occurring Events'. *Journal of Research in Personality*, 37(1), 34–47.

55 Abbey, A. (1982). 'Sex Differences in Attributions for Friendly Behavior: Do Males Misperceive Females' Friendliness?'. *Journal of Personality and Social Psychology*, 42, 830–38; Haselton and Buss (2000).

56 Abbey, A. (1987). 'Misperceptions of Friendly Behavior as Sexual Interest: A Survey of Naturally Occurring Instances'. *Psychology of Women Quarterly*, 11, 173–94.

57 Haselton (2003).

chain store where 13 staff, 12 of whom were women, filed a grievance against their employer.[58] The company had a 'service with a smile' policy, but the predominantly male customers misinterpreted this friendliness as sexual interest. On one occasion, a staff member was forced to hide in a back room to avoid customers, including one who followed her to her car. This incident reveals how the false interpretation of friendly interaction can lead to sexual harassment.

However, this male tendency for excessive optimism can also work against men. It has been suggested that women can exploit this feature of men's nature to achieve other goals. Women can benefit from leading men to believe that they have sexual interest in them. If a man believes that a woman is interested in him, he is more inclined to do favours for her, provide protection or simply give her attention that can boost her confidence and attractiveness to others. Seen in this light, men's sexual over-perception bias can set the stage for both sexual harassment by men and deceptive manipulation by women.[59]

There now exists a large body of research supporting the idea that men over-perceive women's sexual interest. However, we must be careful that we do not exaggerate its influence. Women also make mistakes, and men can improve with experience. There are also other possible causes of confusion. One reason why men may have difficulty reading women's intent may be because women are harder to read than men.

At first glance, it does not make sense that women would be hard to decode. After all, the mating process would go more smoothly if we could read each other's cues that indicate interest. These include language content, tone of voice and non-verbal behaviours such as body language and eye contact.[60] However, as we have noted, women are more cautious. Women, who bear the burden of pregnancy, face greater risks in choosing mates, and because of this may act more covertly and ambiguously during initial interactions. This can make it

---

58 Curtis, K. (1998). 'Safeway Clerks Object to Smile Rule', Associated Press, 2 September, http://www.apnewsarchive.com/1998/Safeway-Clerks-Object-to-Smile-Rule/id-6a186d5d0d7dad468 9dc14e30bd6d3bc, accessed 20 July 2013.

59 Haselton (2003).

60 Ambady, N. and Rosenthal, R. (1992). 'Thin Slices of Expressive Behavior as Predictors of Interpersonal Consequences: A Meta-analysis'. *Psychological Bulletin*, 111, 256–74; Penke, L. and Asendorpf, J.B. (2008). 'Beyond Global Socio-sexual Orientations: A More Differentiated Look at Socio-sexuality and its Effects on Courtship and Romantic Relationships'. *Journal of Personality and Social Psychology*, 95, 1,113–35.

more difficult for men to read their intentions.[61] To test this, one study asked both men and women to judge the level of sexual interest of a sample group containing both sexes.[62] The results indicated that both sexes found it hard to read women's interest levels. Men were relatively easy to read, but predictions of female interest were only slightly above chance. This raises the possibility that women deliberately mask their true intentions.

The research suggests that these gender differences in human nature can contribute to both the conduct and perception of sexual harassment. One interpretation is that the man is led by the flirting to expect a sexual encounter, but grows frustrated and confused when the woman unexpectedly turns down his sexual overtures.[63] While it is understandable that a male responds to flirting by pursuing a woman, it is no excuse for aggression.

Similarly, a man looking for a relationship may feel anger to learn that he has been used for an ego-trip, but it is no justification for harassment. On such occasions, both parties display understandable behaviour. The woman has been flirting to feel good about her appearance, while the man feels he has been led on. As a manager, you may need to advise both parties to modify their behaviour.

Miscommunication is a common source of conflict, and gender differences can contribute to the chances of this happening. Miscommunication occurs when the meaning a receiver reads in a message is different from what the sender intended. Because of gender differences, this can commonly occur. Similarly, if a sender unintentionally sends a message that the receiver interprets as sexual interest, misinterpretation occurs.[64] Finally, if a woman sends a message that she is not interested, but the receiver does not decode the message accurately, perhaps because of previous distortions, there is an increased likelihood of conflict.

Given the prevalence of flirting, it is important to understand the implications of miscommunication.[65] Senders of a message may use sexual allure to achieve other goals. The receiver interprets the message as sexual interest, when in

61 Grammer, K., Kruck. K., Juette, A. and Fink, B. (2000). 'Non-verbal Behavior as Courtship Signals: The Role of Control and Choice in Selecting Partners'. *Evolution and Human Behavior*, 21(6), 371–90; Haselton and Buss (2000).

62 Place, S.S., Todd, P.M., Penke, L. and Asendorpf, J.B. (2009). 'The Ability to Judge the Romantic Interest of Others'. *Psychological Science*, 20(1), 22–6.

63 Kanin, E.J. (1969). 'Selected Dyadic Aspects of Male Sex Aggression'. *Archives of Sex Research*, 5, 12–28.

64 Henningsen (2004).

65 Henningsen, Braz and Davies (2008).

reality, no interest exists. There is a high chance that this can occur, because men seem to have a tendency to interpret flirting as sexually motivated. However, women may be doing it for fun, esteem or relational development.[66]

It appears that men are more likely to perceive women's behaviour as sexual even when flirting isn't happening. In 1982, Abbey conducted a study where men and women observed other people interacting and judged the level of their sexual interest.[67] Abbey found that men are more likely to perceive a woman's actions as sexually motivated even when she is just trying to be friendly. Another distorting factor may appear when a woman has to say 'no'. This can be an uncomfortable moment for the woman, and not wanting to hurt the man's feelings, she may say something ambiguous like, 'I'm not in the mood now.'[68] If the man has previously interpreted interest from their previous interactions, this type of answer will be interpreted as a temporary refusal, and he is likely to continue his approaches.

These misperceptions and miscommunications have implications for harassment. A man has to make a judgement call as to whether a woman is interested, and his judgement is strongly shaped by his previous interpretations. If he previously interpreted the woman's motives as sexual, his expectations will be raised that sex will occur, and this could lead to frustration and anger when he receives a subsequent 'no'. In fact, he may even interpret the woman's decline as hostile, given the previous interactions. The previous interactions create the context in which the rejection is interpreted.

Clearly, it would be wrong to label a man as a sexual harasser if he had no intention of doing so, but was misdirected by these subtle behaviours and natural mis-perceptions, however ignoring them could have one important negative consequence. They could be used to excuse sexual harassment. Sexually aggressive men could rely on miscommunication to absolve their guilt, leaving women exposed and vulnerable.[69] For some men, misinterpretation has nothing to do with their actions. And here a very important point must be stressed: *There is no excuse for harassment*. The goal of management must be to prevent and deal with it in the most appropriate manner, and it is with this goal in mind that this chapter seeks to explore the issue.

---

66 Henningsen (2004).
67 Abbey (1982).
68 McCormick, N.B. (1979). 'Come-ons and Put-offs: Unmarried Students' Strategies for Having and Avoiding Sexual Intercourse'. *Psychology of Women Quarterly*, 4, 194–211.
69 Farris, C., Treat, T.A., Viken, R.J. and McFall, R.M. (2008). 'Sexual Coercion and the Misperception of Sexual Intent'. *Clinical Psychology Review*, 28(1), 48–66.

It must be remembered that when we are looking at the research, we are talking about tendencies, not majority actions. Many men will interpret cues correctly, and many women will not flirt for other motives. On the other hand, there is a sub-group of men who are predisposed to respond to frustration with aggression. In between are men who may misinterpret, and this may lead to actions that women perceive as harassment.

Some men can be completely stupid. In one case brought to court in the United States, a supervisor telephoned several of his female subordinates at home and propositioned them. He also repeatedly engaged in suggestive behaviour at work. The court found that he had a 'total inability to separate his work life from personal matters'.[70]

As a manager, you need to be aware of the full impact of harassment. For a woman who has endured sexual harassment, there can be serious long-term consequences. It can undermine her sense of trust and security long after the harassment has ended. This may even affect her normal romantic interactions. The results can reduce her quality of life for years into the future.

Men's and Women's Perspectives and Justice

Other differences between males and females concern what they believe constitutes harassment. Women are likely to perceive a broader range of behaviours as being harassment, but the difference is not large, and depends on the type of behaviour.[71] Nevertheless there are some behaviours that women perceive as threatening which men think are harmless.

Men and women agree that sexual coercion and sexual propositions constitute harassment.[72] In the case of behaviours defined as physical non-sexual contact, such as congratulatory hugs, both sexes seem to be in agreement that these do not constitute harassment.[73] However, there is less agreement on less extreme and more ambiguous behaviours like displaying derogatory attitudes and dating pressure. Men and women do not always agree that jokes that stereotype gender are harassment. Nor do they agree that repeated requests for dates after being declined are harassment.

---

70 *Toscano* v. *Nimmo*, 570 F. Supp. 1197, 1198 (D. Delaware, 1983).
71 Rotundo, Nguyen and Sackett (2001).
72 Ibid.
73 Gutek, B.A. and O'Connor, M. (1995). 'The Empirical Basis for the Reasonable Woman Standard'. *Journal of Social Issues*, 51, 151–66.

There is also a big difference in behaviours described as physical sexual contact. Women are more likely to perceive sexual touching as sexual harassment.[74] For example Gutek (1985) found that 59 per cent of men interpreted it as harassment, compared to 89 per cent of women.[75] The majority of both men and women see it as harassment, but men are more likely to view physical sexual contact as a compliment. Women tend to see it as intrusive and threatening.

Differences in interpretation have important implications for sexual harassment – do you adopt the man's or the woman's perspective? There are very good reasons for adopting the woman's perspective. If procedures are dealt with from a man's perspective, it may discourage women from reporting complaints.[76] Early studies have shown that cases are under-reported. For example, for the 1982–83 academic year, academic institutions averaged only 4.3 complaints.[77] This is a very low figure given that around the same time, 20–30 per cent of female college students reported experiencing sexual harassment.[78] A second concern arises from findings that show men are also more likely than women to blame women for being sexually harassed.[79]

Becker (1967) suggests that another reason for taking the woman's perspective is because of the dominance of men in leadership positions, which will bias policy and interpretation towards men.[80] Attribution Theory can help explain this. Attribution Theory suggests that if something goes wrong in our own lives, we will tend to blame the circumstances at the time. However, if something goes wrong with another person, we tend to attribute the cause to their personality or other internal characteristics. Men are more likely to see a case of sexual harassment through the eyes of the male and to attribute his actions to the situation including provocation. Women, on the other hand, are more likely to perceive the case through the eyes of the victim.[81]

74 Rotundo, Nguyen and Sackett (2001).
75 Gutek, B. (1985). *Sex and the Workplace*, San Francisco, CA: Jossey-Bass.
76 Riger, S. (1991). 'Gender Dilemmas in Sexual Harassment Policies and Procedures'. *American Psychologist*, 46(5), 497–505.
77 Robertson, C., Dyer, C.E. and Campbell, D. (1988). 'Campus Harassment: Sexual Harassment Policies and Procedures at Institutions of Higher Learning'. *Signs: Journal of Women in Culture and Society*, 13(4), 792–812.
78 Dzeich, B. and Weiner, L. (1984). *The Lecherous Professor: Sexual Harassment on Campus*, Boston, MA: Beacon Press.
79 Kenig, S. and Ryan, J. (1986). 'Sex Differences in Levels of Tolerance and Attribution of Blame for Sexual Harassment on a University Campus'. *Sex Roles*, 15, 535–49.
80 Becker, H. (1967). 'Whose Side are We On?'. *Social Problems*, 14, 239–48.
81 Riger (1991).

In light of these facts, Rigor argued that 'policymakers and others need to learn to think like a woman to define which behaviours constitute harassment'.[82] Given the inherent logic in these arguments, the US courts did in fact begin to think like a woman. In 1991, landmark rulings saw the courts adopting 'the reasonable woman standard', which requires decision-makers to adopt the perspective of the harassee, who in most cases is a woman. However, Rotundo, Nguyen and Sackett note: 'the courts made the decision to implement the reasonable woman standard without any conclusive evidence about the magnitude of the assumed gender difference'.[83]

Given the existence of these gender differences, it has been argued that the reasonable woman standard may be unfair to men.[84] When a reasonable woman determines what is at fault, a reasonable man may find himself guilty even though he had no intention of causing offence. For example, if he complimented a woman's appearance, he may have been motivated by good intentions. However, if the law was changed back to a reasonable person standard, which tried to consider both genders' viewpoints, we might see guilty men exploiting miscommunication as a defence for inappropriate behaviour. However, males are not the only gender with its share of manipulators. For example, if two workers have had a consensual relationship, it is not unusual to see a false claim of harassment when that relationship comes to an end.[85]

The work environment has changed dramatically since Becker wrote in 1967. Women are now in more positions of power, particularly in human resource departments which commonly deal with harassment cases. In fact, it may be that these changes have created a significant bias against men. Consider the following experience of a man who previously worked as a college tutor:

> *I taught at a tertiary college which allowed dating if both partners consented. I began dating Maggie, an ex-student who was no longer in my class but was still at the college. As I got to know her, I discovered she had a history of psychological problems and false accusations. Sure enough, when we stopped going out, she accused me of forcing her in to 14 dates against her will.*

---

82 Ibid., p. 503.
83 Rotundo, Nguyen and Sackett (2001), p. 914.
84 Meads, M.A. (1993). 'Applying the Reasonable Woman Standard in Evaluating Sexual Harassment Claims: Is it Justified?'. *Law and Psychology Review*, 17, 209–23.
85 Leahy, J.T. (1999). 'Regulating Workplace Relationships'. *Boxboard Containers International*, 106(7), 17.

> The Harassment Officer conducted a review and reported that
> my chief witness said 'Maggie was going through hell' with me. I was
> stunned as I had expected the witness to support me. How could I get it
> so wrong? This was the last day I hugged my niece.
>
> Some months later, I ran into the witness and asked her why she
> said Maggie was going through hell with me. She responded 'I didn't.
> I said Maggie was going through hell, full stop.' She explained that
> she meant Maggie was going through hell in all aspects of her life
> because she was so crazy.
>
> The officer who falsely recorded the comment had devoted her life to
> feminist and lesbian causes.

While we can admire people who fight for the rights of women, the question raised in the above case is whether such a person can equally empathize with both parties. In this case, the Harassment Officer's concern with perceived power in the relationship took priority over accuracy of reporting. It is quite common for Harassment Officers to be people with a concern for women's issues, but harassment affects both genders, and both have a right to procedural justice. A notable aspect of the description above is the teacher's comment, 'This was the last day I hugged my niece' – a reminder that managerial actions can have huge consequences for employees' private lives.

As a manager, you must protect the dignity of your workers, regardless of their gender. The options open to a manager on receiving a harassment claim are similar to those when dealing with a bullying claim. For minor cases, informal options can focus on problem-solving. Instead of trying to prove guilt or innocence, this approach focuses on preventing the problem occurring again in future. This approach assumes that both parties want the problem solved and believe it can be done by working through the issue. For example, it may require a male to recognize that his behaviour is causing offence and agreeing to not repeat it in the future. No disciplinary action is taken.

More serious cases will generate a formal procedure. These generally require a written complaint and are more adversarial in nature. Typically, each party has to persuade a hearing board of the strength of their case. If found guilty, the harasser may be punished. However, these procedures may discourage a woman from making a complaint as she may fear retaliation, particularly if the person she is accusing has more power. It is important that your staff have faith in the organization's ability to protect them.

Once again, the best option for a manager is pre-emption, with well-publicized policies, informal and formal resolution mechanisms, a contact person and a culture of respect. Not only does this reduce the time you spend dealing with such cases, it reduces the chances that your staff will endure unwanted behaviour and a reduction in quality of life.

8

Could You Be a Hypocrite and Not Know It?

> *No man is clever enough to know all the evil he does.*
> *François de la Rochefoucauld*[1]

An academic described her department manager:

> *On the eve of his retirement, Ron gave his farewell speech in which he stated how, in his time as manager, he stood for fairness, staff and family.*
>
> *The same day that he gave his speech, I asked to look at my personal file, and discovered that some time earlier, Ron had placed documents criticizing me for taking leave without pay. I had taken the leave to visit my dying mother. The hospital had phoned me suggesting I come down straight away. I didn't think it would be a problem as it was a Friday and most staff did not come in on Fridays. Nevertheless, I was disciplined.*
>
> *Ironically, when Ron's wife got sick, he would stay away for weeks on end.*

Among many of the staff, Ron had a reputation as a bully. He seemed to take pleasure in seeing conflict between his staff and, for example, did not enforce company policies regarding offensive emails. Yet Ron prided himself on his sense of social responsibility. He had even co-edited a book on the subject. How could he be such a hypocrite?

Situational factors may have impacted on Ron's self-perception. In Chapter 5, we saw how leaders often develop in-groups and out-groups among their staff.

---

1   De la Rochefoucauld, F. (1871). *Reflections; Or Sentences and Moral Maxims by Francois Duc De La Rochefoucauld, Prince de Marsillac,* transl. J.W. Willis Bund and J. Hain Friswell, London: Simpson Low, Son, and Marston.

We would expect in-groups to provide managers with positive feedback about their performance. The staff members who support you may become trusted workers, and the similarity in their workplace schema makes these workers appear highly rational. In contrast, those workers who disagree with you appear illogical, and you have to accept that every workforce has its problem workers who are never satisfied.

This illustrates one of the problems you may encounter as a manager. Your actions might not be perfect, but you have limited time and resources. You can only do your best under the conditions at the time. All managers have a limited span of absolute judgement, and sometimes you will make mistakes. This means your performance will never be perfect. You can only do your best, and that means you cannot satisfy everyone.

Ron's inability to see his own faults reflects common cognitive distortions that we humans make, and it raises a very important question: Could you be a hypocrite and not know it? To explore this issue in more depth, we should re-phrase the question and ask, 'How could Ron have such an inaccurate self-concept?' How could he not see the difference between what he was and what he prescribed? The answer to this is important for maintaining ethical standards among your workforce and avoiding hypocrisy. In Chapter 2, we explained how self-esteem and self-identity are two core motives. In this section, we will discover how these concepts can distort self-perception and lead to unethical behaviour.

Hypocrisy as a Psychological Process

In 1989, Kunda and Sanitioso conducted two studies in which subjects were first led to believe that a certain personal attribute was likely to lead to positive outcomes.[2] For example, they were told that people with introverted personality characteristics were likely to gain certain benefits in life. On hearing this, extroverted people began to view themselves as less extroverted and somewhat more introverted. This research revealed how our self-perception is shaped by what other people consider to be important values.

It is important to note that the subjects didn't just start saying they were more introverted, they actually found evidence to back up their views.

2   Kunda, Z. and Sanitioso, R. (1989). 'Motivated Changes in the Self-concept'. *Journal of Experimental Social Psychology*, 25, 272–85.

They searched their memories for evidence that they possessed the desired attributes. Of course, a memory search may throw up conflicting information, so their self-concepts could only change as far as their prior self-knowledge would allow. Nevertheless, changes in self-perception did occur.

This study has since been supported by a number of others which show that how we perceive ourselves is strongly influenced by what society values. We often look for and present personal qualities in ourselves that society finds desirable.[3] The link between distorted self-perception and moral judgements is not new. In the eighteenth century, Adam Smith, the father of economics, noted how 'self-love' and a desire for 'propriety' in our behaviour distorted our moral judgements. In his *Theory of Moral Sentiments*, Smith wrote: 'so partial are the views of mankind with regard to the propriety of their own conduct, both at the time of action and after it; and so difficult is it for them to view it in the light in which any indifferent spectator would consider it'.[4]

Our desire to appear righteous means we do not perceive our behaviour as impartially as an independent observer. This has important implications for ethical behaviour and the teaching of business ethics. We need to ask how society's values are distorting our self-perception, and we may even need to consider the possibility that a strong emphasis on ethics may be counterproductive, as it distorts our self-concept and may lead to hypocrisy. It suggests we need to change the emphasis from teaching ethics to teaching self-knowing and awareness of the cognitive biases that we can all fall prey to.

Humans may have cognitive limitations, but they are not completely stupid. At some point, we would expect people to discover that they are not acting consistently with their beliefs. This discovery creates cognitive dissonance. You will recall that cognitive dissonance is the situation in which people have two incompatible thoughts, which creates discomfort or dissonance. We would expect this discomfort to motivate people to change their behaviour. In fact, a number of studies have used a deliberately heightened sense of dissonance to motivate people to act consistently with their beliefs.[5] Seen in this light,

3   Sedikides, C. and Strube, M.J. (1997). 'Self-evaluation: To Thine Own Self Be Good, To Thine Own Self Be Sure, To Thine Own Self Be True, and To Thine Own Self Be Better', in M.P. Zanna (ed.), *Advances in Experimental Social Psychology*, vol. 29, New York: Academic Press, pp. 209–69.

4   Smith, A. (1767). *Theory of Moral sentiments*, 3rd edn, Edinburgh: Millar, Kincaid and Bell, p. 222.

5   Fried, C. and Aronson, E. (1995). 'Hypocrisy, Misattribution, and Dissonance Reduction'. *Personality and Social Psychology Bulletin*, 21(9), 925–33.

dissonance can be a very positive force, at it motivates people to act with higher ethical standards.[6]

It can be very painful to discover a significant discrepancy between your behaviour and your self-concept. For example, a 2008 study of 7,905 members of the American College of Surgeons found that 6.3 per cent had thought about committing suicide in the previous year. Many of these had discovered they had not met their own performance standards. There was a strong link between making a major error at work and thoughts of suicide: 16.2 per cent of surgeons who had made a recent major error considered suicide, compared with 5.4 per cent who hadn't.[7]

When we discover that our behaviour does not comply with our ideals, it can dramatically affect our psychological welfare, reduce our self-esteem, affect our sense of identity and undermine our faith in our ability to do our job. And in some cases, it can threaten our will to live. The situation is made worse if you believe that everyone else is consistently performing at a higher level. It can be hard to acknowledge our failings, and it is no surprise that cognitive distortions occur to keep ourselves happy. In an influential article, Anand, Ashforth and Joshi (2004) noted that corruption scandals at venerated companies like Enron, Worldcom and Parmalat had some features in common.[8] In particular, the employees who conducted fraudulent acts were not what we would expect in such cases. They were upstanding members of their communities, caring parents and givers to charity. One of the most intriguing aspects is that white-collar criminals do not view themselves as corrupt. They acknowledge that their behaviour was errant, but deny criminal intent and resist being labelled a criminal. Even though they were performing corrupt acts, they maintained their self-concept as ethical people. This raises the question of why cognitive dissonance doesn't motivate them to change this behaviour.

It seems that white-collar criminals resolve this dissonance through other means. They rationalize their actions. Anand, Ashforth and Joshi state: 'Rationalizations are mental strategies that allow employees (and others around

---

6   Aronson, E., Fried, C. and Stone, J. (1991). 'Overcoming Denial and Increasing the Intention to Use Condoms through the Induction of Hypocrisy'. *American Journal of Public Health*, 81(12), 1,636–8.
7   HealthDay (2011). 'Many Surgeons Have Contemplated Suicide, Study Finds', 18 January, http://health.usnews.com/health-news/family-health/brain-and-behavior/articles/2011/01/18/many-surgeons-have-contemplated-suicide-study-finds, accessed 20 July 2013.
8   Anand, V., Ashforth, B.E. and Joshi, M. (2004). 'Business as Usual: The Acceptance and Perpetuation of Corruption in Organizations'. *Academy of Management Executive*, 18(2), 39–53.

them) to view their corrupt actions as justified. Employees may collectively use rationalizations to neutralize any regrets or negative feelings that emanate from their participation in unethical acts.'[9] They identified a number of rationalization tactics, some of which are explored below.

DENIAL OF RESPONSIBILITY

This occurs when individuals convince themselves that they had no real choice but to act in a corrupt manner, possibly because of the circumstances at the time, or perhaps due to pressure from superiors. In such cases, they do not link their behaviour to their self-identity, so there is no cognitive dissonance. Instead, they see themselves as moral people being forced into unethical acts.

DENIAL OF INJURY

In some cases, people justify their unethical behaviour by saying: 'No one is really harmed by my actions, and therefore my actions are not really corrupt.' An example of this is where an employee steals from their boss, but says it's OK because the organization is insured. Another approach is to say it's not bad because other people are doing much worse. They compare their unethical behaviour to more extreme forms which make their behaviour look mellow in comparison.

DENIAL OF VICTIM

In these cases, individuals justify their actions by saying that someone deserved to be a victim, perhaps pointing out problems in the victim's behaviour. It may even reach the point where the victim is dehumanized. This can be seen in accounts of Wall Street traders who did not view their clients as individuals, but as suckers waiting to be conned.

BALANCING THE LEDGER

In these cases, the human tendency towards reciprocity is drawn on to justify immoral behaviour. The perpetrator may believe that they have done such a good job for their company that they deserve a little extra. Or alternatively, they may feel harmed, in which case, their unethical behaviour was merely re-balancing the ledger.

---

9   Ibid., p. 39.

SOCIAL WEIGHTING

This can occur in two different forms. The first is to say that their behaviour is not immoral because the law is wrong. We can see this in the actions of people who illegally download material from the Internet. They may argue that the law is wrong (despite the fact that their actions deprive producers of income for their work). Another form of social weighting is similar to 'denial of injury' described above, in which individuals avoid building up negative impressions of themselves by comparing themselves to others who commit even worse behaviours. Their social comparison makes them look better than they are.

APPEAL TO HIGHER LOYALTIES

This occurs where individuals argue that some unethical behaviours are required because the overall goal is so important. This can be seen in the policeman who doesn't follow the rules, but believes his methods are necessary to keep the peace. In major cases of corporate corruption, it can be seen in attitudes like 'We do this because we are saving this great firm,' or 'We do this because we are saving our great economy.' In such cases, perpetrators over-rationalize so that the higher goal is seen as more important than simple unlawful acts.[10]

EVERYONE IS DOING IT

Another common rationalization is where individuals claim that 'everyone is doing it', thereby reducing the perception of the behaviour as unethical.[11]

One problem identified by researchers is the way that corruption can escalate beyond the control of the individuals involved. If left unchecked, the initial act of corruption, whether it be deception, theft, fraud or anything else, can increase in size and scope.[12] Consider the example of the accounting company Arthur Andersen, whose deceptive accounting processes helped lead to the collapse of Enron. Their company motto was 'Think straight, talk straight'. For many decades, the company was highly principled, but at some point deceptive practices crept in and escalated uncontrollably. In such cases, corruption soars in scale and scope, and takes on a momentum of its own.

---

10 Zyglidopoulos, S.C., Fleming, P.J. and Rothenberg, S. (2008). 'Rationalization, Overcompensation and the Escalation of Corruption in Organizations'. *Journal of Business Ethics*, 84, Supplement 1, 65–73.
11 Rossouw, G.J., Mulder, L. and Barkhuysen, B. (2000). 'Defining and Understanding Fraud: A South African Case Study'. *Business Ethics Quarterly*, 10(4), 885–95.
12 Zyglidopoulos, Fleming and Rothenberg (2008).

Arthur Anderson was one of the five largest accounting and auditing partnerships in the world. One of its major clients was the Texas-based energy company Enron, which exploited accounting loopholes, misrepresented earnings and modified its balance sheet to inflate asset values and reduce liabilities. Many of the senior executives at Enron were found guilty and imprisoned for offences that included fraud, money laundering, conspiracy and insider trading.

An ex-Enron executive explained how the rationalization of behaviour became the norm: 'You did it once, it smelled bad ... you did it again, it didn't smell as bad.'[13] Having got away with the first case of lying, it is not so hard to do it again. This reduces the perception of risk, and individuals find it easier to lie again. Secondly, additional lies may be necessary to hide the first one, in which case deception increases. As deception escalates, it can come to pervade the organization as more individuals get involved. It may even become sanctioned by an authority figure.[14]

If corrupt behaviours become widespread, the organization's socialization processes can cause newcomers to adopt those behaviours.[15] When newcomers arrive and are confronted by these practices, they may be tempted to quit, but this can actually increase corruption by weeding out any who are resistant to them. In the socialization phase, newcomers may find that unethical behaviour leads to higher rewards. They may be introduced to corrupt behaviours incrementally, initially performing a task that is slightly deviant which they have no trouble rationalizing. Once they accept that practice as normal, they are exposed to more practices. In some cases, they may adopt the corrupt practices in an attempt to resolve dilemmas and conflicts in their workplace. The corrupt behaviour is not the best solution, but it is a compromise that solves a problem.

The extent to which new workers buy in to these behaviours is influenced by the attractiveness of the group they are joining. If membership of a group is highly prized, newcomers are more likely to accept the behaviours. This could be seen at Arthur Anderson, where new recruits were led to believe that membership of the company was exclusive and special.[16] Newcomers were willing to emulate the experienced staff who mentored them.

13 McLean, B. and Elkind, P. (2003). *The Smartest Guys in the Room: The Amazing Rise and Scandalous Fall of Enron*, New York: Penguin Books, p. 128.
14 Fleming, P. and Zyglidopoulos, S.C. (2008). 'The Escalation of Deception in Organizations'. *Journal of Business Ethics*, 81(4), 837–50.
15 Anand, Ashforth and Joshi (2004).
16 Ibid.

Another factor affecting the extent to which new workers accept the practices they are taught is the extent to which a group is socially cocooned and develops it own cultural norms. The organization may even use language that reduces the sense of wrongdoing. For example, in the 1950s, radio disc jockeys were routinely bribed by record companies to play music for them – but they were not called bribes, but 'auditioning fees'.[17]

Could You Fall into Unethical Behaviour Patterns without Knowing It?

You might think that some behaviours are so obviously bad that you will never commit them. However, sometimes people fall in to traps by following a line of thinking that overlooks the obvious. Consider the example of Dennis Gioia.[18] Gioia had high moral standards. As a university student during the 1960s, he was dismayed at the unethical decision-making that, for example, led to the US involvement in the Vietnam War. Nor did he approve of many of the business practices of the day, which he believed lacked ethical standards:

> To me the typical stance of business seemed to be one of disdain for, rather than responsibility toward, the society of which they were prominent members. I wanted something to change. Accordingly, I cultivated my social awareness; I held my principles high; I espoused my intention to help a troubled world.[19]

On graduation, Gioia got a job with the Ford Motor Company, and by the summer of 1973 was appointed Ford's Recall Manager. In this role, he co-ordinated the recall of cars with problems, as well as tracking incoming information to identify any new problems. At the time of his appointment, there were about a hundred recall campaigns in action, most related to safety.

One of the new problems that came to his attention concerned the Pinto model of car, which could burst into flames in rear-end accidents. However, Gioia did not deem it important enough to justify a recall. It is important to stress that all recall campaigns involve life and death, but in the case of the Pinto, the problems did not occur frequently enough to justify a recall, and the causes were not directly traceable: 'We could not recall all cars with potential problems and stay in business.'

---

17 Ibid.
18 Gioia, D.A. (1992). 'Pinto Fires and Personal Ethics: A Script Analysis of Missed Opportunities'. *Journal of Business Ethics*, 11(5–6), 379–89.
19 Ibid., p. 379.

On 10 August 1978, three teenage girls were burned alive when their Pinto was hit from behind by a van, focusing national attention on the car. By this stage, Gioia had left the job, but he was haunted by the fact that he had not acted:

> *After I left Ford I now argue and teach that Ford had an ethical obligation to recall. But, while I was there, I perceived no strong obligation to recall and I remember no strong ethical overtones to the case whatsoever. It was a very straightforward decision, driven by dominant scripts for the time, place, and context.*[20]

So how did he get it so wrong? This is an important case that illustrates that ethical people can make bad decisions. The first thing to remember is the cognitive limitations discussed in Chapter 2 – in particular, our limited span of absolute judgement. There is a limit to how much information we can rationally maximize. With this in mind, Gioia's description of his work is enlightening:

> *It is difficult to convey the overwhelming complexity and pace of the job of keeping track of so many active or potential recall campaigns. It remains the busiest, most information-filled job I have ever held or would want to hold …. In this office everything is a crisis.*[21]

To allow us to handle such high workloads, we normally follow procedures and ways of thinking taught to us when we start the job. Gioia calls these 'script schemas', a 'cognitive framework that people use to impose structure upon information situations and expectations to facilitate understanding'. Gioia had been trained how to analyse and process the information he received, and none of the reports on the Pinto had features that would normally raise his concern. He had seen this sort of information hundreds of times before. They were normal accidents. Other reports were more serious:

> *The overwhelming information overload that characterized the role as well as its hectic pace actually forced a greater reliance on scripted responses. It was impossible to handle the job requirements without relying on some sort of automatic way of assessing whether a case deserved active attention. There was so much to do and so much information to attend to that the only way to deal with it was by means of schematic processing.*[22]

---

20 Ibid., p. 388.
21 Ibid., p. 382.
22 Ibid., p. 386.

Gioia's experience shows that with high levels of information and limited human cognitive abilities, ethical people can make poor decisions. We sometimes follow patterns of thinking that overlook important issues.

The implication of the research described above is that all humans have the potential to perform unethical behaviours, and we are all capable of being hypocrites. If the situation is right, our human tendencies may take us to places where we don't want to go. This does not mean we should lower our standards. On the contrary, it highlights the importance of imposing ethical controls. Failure to do so can result in expensive litigation, while some forms of unethical behaviour, like fraud or theft, can cost the company dearly.

In some cases the, unethical behaviour occurs because a staff member has an upbringing and social schema that supports unethical behaviour. In other cases, good people can also act unethically. You as a manager must have precautions in place to cater for all possibilities. A number of options exist to counter unethical behaviour. They include the following:

1.   **Identify areas of high risk** – Identify units or processes in the organization with characteristics that leave them open to unethical practices.

2.   **Develop additional controls** – Controls can be introduced to reduce the opportunity to act corruptly. This includes security and access controls to reduce theft, and audits of processes.

3.   **Detect corruption** – The earlier unethical behaviour is discovered, the less costly it is. Surprise audits and performance reviews can help to uncover such behaviour.

4.   **Provide safe avenues for whistle-blowers** – Create safe means to allow tipsters to report unethical behaviour they discover to management.[23]

5.   **Develop a code of ethics** – A corporate code of ethics sends a powerful message to staff regarding management expectations of appropriate behaviour.[24]

---

23 Marks, J. (2009). 'Uncovering Hidden Risks'. *Financial Executive*, 25(5), 44–7.
24 Stevens, B. (1994). 'An Analysis of Corporate Ethical Code Studies: Where Do We Go From Here?'. *Journal of Business Ethics*, 13, 63–9.

6.   **Ensure fair management practice**s – Research has shown that employees who believe they have been treated unfairly are more likely to participate in deviant behaviour.[25] In a variation of the reciprocity principle, employees may feel motivated to seek revenge.[26] If managers act fairly in their day-to-day activities, they are less likely to cause resentment that gives rise to such behaviour.

7.   **Provide moral education** – There is an important role for moral education about the negative impacts of unethical behaviour.[27]

The last item above, moral education, must be quantified, as earlier in this chapter we raised the possibility that moral education could be counterproductive. The question that needs to be answered is: 'Does ethical education change behaviour or self-concept?' Unfortunately, there has been little research on this. If it does change self-concept, it may increase unethical behaviour. This may require a change from nebulous education, which stresses that people should be good, to education about more specific examples of temptation. It also suggests that we need more education on self-knowing and how difficult it is to acknowledge our limitations. We must be made aware of how easy it is to fall into unethical behavioural traps. The role of business educators and managers alike must change to make it easier for employees to acknowledge their weaknesses and the cognitive processes involved.

Know Thyself

> As I grow older, I discover more and more aspects of my personality that I don't like. These are not features I recently acquired. They are long held characteristics that I have recently become aware of – Why didn't I see them earlier?

In olden days, there were seven Greek sages who were gifted in the art of concise words. With very few words, they could create simple sayings of great

25   Kickul, J. (2001). 'When Organizations Break their Promises: Employee Reactions to Unfair Process and Treatments'. *Journal of Business Ethics*, 29, 289–307.

26   Bies, R.J. and Tripp, T.M. (2001). 'A Passion for Justice: The Rationality and Morality', in R. Cropanzano (ed.), *Justice in the Workplace*, 2nd edn, Hillsdale, NJ: Lawrence Erlbaum Associates, pp. 197–208.

27   Rossouw, Mulder and Barkhuysen (2000).

force. According to legend, the seven wise men met at the oracle at Delphi and the Temple of Apollo, and inscribed two words: 'Know thyself.' These words have challenged the world's greatest Greek philosophers, including Plato and Socrates, who spent time trying to decipher what the sages were saying. Socrates noted how ridiculous it was that people try to gain obscure knowledge before they know themselves. Plato also thought that understanding yourself was important to understanding human nature.

The ancient Greeks believed we should strive to understand our actions, motivations and feelings. However, the more we know ourselves, the more we discover our limitations. This means that it is not enough to just know ourselves, we must also accept ourselves. We must recognize the normality of these limitations. People who think they do not possess such limitations have an inaccurate view of themselves and human nature, and this will limit their ability to manage.

However, modern psychology shows us that it is hard to know ourselves. We have so many cognitive biases and perceptual limitations that we have a limited, if not distorted, self-perception. Our motivation for self-esteem further inflates our self-concept. Herein lies the problem: it is hard to know our limitations because our limitations make it hard to know ourselves.

The superior manager or person is not without negative tendencies, as all humans have them. This places the onus not on appearing to be a superior person, but on actively discovering your negative tendencies and under what conditions they are likely to appear. Then you must develop strategies to control them. Knowing yourself and your negative tendencies is the starting point for becoming a superior manager.

The main reason we don't see our faults is not because we are blind or stupid. It is because they often operate below our level of consciousness. We are not always aware when cognitive dissonance or social comparison affects our judgement. We are not always conscious that self-esteem is influencing our behaviour. We need to develop greater understanding of ourselves, and an ability to self-critique, but this is a skill that takes time to cultivate.

A task I give my leadership students is to keep a diary of their workplace interactions. They must explore their interactions of the previous day, looking for characteristics from our model of human nature in themselves and others. They then re-evaluate their own actions in the same way that a football coach will analyse a video of a game just played. It provides an opportunity to re-evaluate their conversations and the motives behind them. A principal task of management educators in the future is to find better ways to enable people to discover and accept their limitations.

A New Approach to Social Responsibility

Ethics and social responsibility are a routine part of business education today. The prevailing argument is that managers need to consider the effects of their actions on broader society. However, this book takes a different view of social responsibility, arguing that if managers truly want to make society a better place to live, they should begin by being better managers. Managers are the heads of small communities, and their behaviour can have a significant impact on the welfare of those people.

The workplace puts managers in positions where they will have to deal with conflicting needs and expectations. Problems with our bosses at work rank as the second-highest sources of conflict in our lives, behind those we have with our spouses.[28] Sadly, it is not just unrealistic worker expectations that cause these conflicts. A study of 468 leaders in New Zealand found that many top-level executives displayed attitudes that were so unconstructive they hurt the company.[29] For example, 13 per cent championed competitiveness between their staff, developing a 'win–lose' framework that encouraged staff to manipulate situations to enhance their position. The study found that 38 per cent used pessimistic leadership behaviours, such as always pointing out mistakes and encouraging staff to criticize others. A large minority (21 per cent) even encouraged staff to avoid blame by shifting responsibility to others.[30]

Positive and negative feelings that workers experience in the workplace can spill over into other areas of their life. In some cases, workers can tolerate poor workplace experiences if other factors compensate. For example, they may endure a horrible boss and work conditions if they are paid very well. The compensation allows people to stay happy in their daily life despite

---

28 Argyle, M. and Henderson, M. (1985). *The Anatomy of Relationships*, London: Heinemann, p. 258.

29 Harris, C. (2009). 'Negative Attitudes to Staff Harm Firms'. *The Dominion Post*, 28 November.

30 McCarthy, S. (2009). *The Leadership Culture Performance Connection: Transforming Leadership and Culture – the State of the Nations*, Plymouth, MI: Human Synergistics.

the job. However, for most of us, there is a strong link between our jobs and life satisfaction.[31]

The link between happiness at work and the rest of our life runs both ways. In the same way that happiness at work affects our happiness outside work, our overall happiness can influence our satisfaction with our job.[32] Happier people are healthier, more socially engaged and more successful.[33]

A study by Wright and Bonett confirmed the importance of a happy workforce.[34] To assess well-being, managers were asked a series of questions, such as how often they felt 'very lonely or remote from other people', 'depressed or very unhappy' and 'on top of the world'. They were also asked questions about job performance, job satisfaction and turnover. The results showed a positive relationship between personal well-being and job satisfaction. As we might expect, there was also a link between performance and well-being. Those doing well in their jobs were happier, although the link between job satisfaction and job performance was not so strong. As expected, there was a negative link between turnover and both well-being and job satisfaction.

The study also found that workers with low levels of well-being are more likely to leave their jobs. Poor performers are likely to leave their jobs if they feel they are not doing well in them. However, artificially propping up poor workers is not a good solution, as very good performers will consider leaving if their rewards are disproportionate to their efforts. The good performers may feel that they can do better elsewhere. Wright and Bonett argue that strategies 'should be designed to induce the highest performing employees to stay while encouraging weaker performers to leave'.[35] However, a more constructive approach would be to focus on improving the performance of the poor performers.

When people receive poor evaluations of their work performance, they are more likely to be stressed, and this can encourage them to find a new job. This might be welcomed by a manager who is happy to see a poor performer leave.

---

31 Wright, T.A, Bennett, K.K. and Dun, T. (1999). 'Life and Job Satisfaction'. *Psychological Reports*, 84, 1,025–8.
32 Ibid.
33 Lyubomirsky, S., King, L. and Diener, E. (2005). 'The Benefits of Frequent Positive Affect: Does Happiness Lead to Success?'. *Psychological Bulletin*, 131(6), 803–55.
34 Wright, T.A. and Bonett, D.G. (2007). 'Job Satisfaction and Psychological Well-being as Non-additive Predictors of Workplace Turnover'. *Journal of Management*, 33(2), 141–60.
35 Ibid.

However, it may be that the person is performing badly because you are a bad manager and you have not created a managerial framework that allows your workers to achieve their potential. In this case, their poor performance and departure is not indicative of their ability, but of your managerial performance. This suggests a need for constructive management, which focuses on capability development, constructive feedback and the building of self-esteem, identity and belonging in the workplace.

Motivation theories to extract more effort from workers are regularly taught in management courses, but could those same theories be used to extract more happiness? It seems logical to expect that workers who have satisfying work relationships and are self-actualized are likely to work harder, but not all of the research bears this out. One of the pivotal theories in management is Herzberg's theory that differentiates satisfaction and motivators. Hertzberg revealed that some aspects of work may leave us more satisfied, but they do not necessary make us work harder.

When managers are asked to consider happiness in the workplace, it is normally claimed that happiness leads to increased productivity. Similarly, employees and unions can use this argument to obtain more benefits for workers.[36] Since the establishment of the Human Relations Movement in the 1930s, there has been an expectation that a happy worker is a productive worker. However, research in the 1970s threw cold water on this. The studies on happiness in the workforce could not produce a conclusive finding that happy workers work harder. Part of this may be because of differences in measurement and definition. For example, does happiness correlate to job satisfaction, and what is the relationship between short-term differences in productivity and enduring increases in happiness? The study of the link between satisfaction and performance has become so established that it has been called the 'holy grail' of industrial psychologists.[37] However, despite seventy years of research, uncertainty remains concerning whether happier workers are in fact more productive.[38] Fisher (2003) reviewed the literature on the link between job satisfaction and job performance, and found that there is a positive link, but it is weak.[39]

---

36 Ledford Jr, G.E. (1999). 'Happiness and Productivity Revisited'. *Journal of Organizational Behavior*, 20(1), 25–30.
37 Landy, F.J. (1989). *Psychology of Work Behaviour*, Pacific Grove, CA.: Brooks Cole.
38 Zelenski, J.M., Murphy S.A. and Jenkins, D.A. (2008). 'The Happy-productive Worker Thesis Revisited'. *Journal of Happiness Studies*, 9, 521–37.
39 Fisher, C.D. (2003). 'Why Do Lay People Believe that Satisfaction and Performance are Correlated? Possible Sources of a Commonsense Theory'. *Journal of Organizational Behavior*, 24, 753–77.

A body of research conducted by social psychologists has examined whether people perform better at a task when put in a good mood. The results show that this is indeed the case, although they vary depending on the task.[40] This would suggest that it is in the interests of employers to keep their staff happy. However, research from psychologists also suggests that the link between productivity and happiness may run the other way. It may be that productive workers become happier *because* of their good performance. When people receive positive feedback about their performance, they become happier. In laboratory studies, people given false feedback saying they were doing a good job experienced increased levels of happiness.

This suggests that managers should not seek to make their staff happy to increase productivity. Instead, they should help their staff become more productive, and this will make their staff happier. This implies that you give workers constructive feedback about their performance. This is supported by a large body of research which suggests that individuals who show competence at work feel happier, both in the long term and short term.[41] For example, Staw, Sutton and Pelled (1994) found that individuals who had improved evaluations from their supervisors over an 18-month period experienced and expressed positive emotions.[42]

In this light, we should recall the example of the rental agency in Chapter 4, where the worker quit after discovering she had performed badly. The experience affected her confidence in her ability to do her job, and she decided to leave the industry. This raises the role that good management and staff training can play in raising self-esteem and identity, with important consequences for happiness.

One cause of uncertainty in the research comes from our level of understanding of what causes happiness. For example, there is a large body of research showing that personality traits are a major determinant of an individual's welfare. This trait approach recognizes that some people are naturally happier than others, regardless of what is going on around them. Following this line of reasoning, Ledford (1999) argued that if 'only trait-based

---

40 See Fisher (2003) for a summary.
41 See Fisher (2003) for a summary.
42 Staw, B.M., Sutton, R.I. and Pelled, L.H. (1994). 'Employee Positive Emotion and Favorable Outcomes at the Workplace'. *Organization Science*, 5(1), 51–71.

happiness leads to performance it was pointless to try to make employees happier as a way of improving performance'.[43]

Ledford is not alone in this. Drawing on research that shows that people's happiness levels stay relatively constant over the long term, James Liszka from the University of Alaska states that making decisions to increase happiness has no effect. Humans have a constant level of happiness over time that they seem to revert to. Consequently, trying to increase happiness 'is bad policy criteria and bad ethics'. However, Liska also notes that 'there are some events in life that are such that no amount of optimism overcomes'.[44] Managers may have a significant impact at any point in time.

While we might not be able to prove a link between happiness and productivity, it is easier to find a link between happiness and attendance at work. Curkendall et al. (2010) found that workers suffering from depression are more likely to claim sick leave than their healthy colleagues.[45] A happy workforce is also likely to reduce the cost of turnover. In their book *The Dissatisfied Worker*, Fisher and Hanna noted that low employee well-being was responsible for a high level of turnover.[46] Employees leave their jobs for any number of reasons, but job satisfaction is a significant cause[47] – a finding supported by a large body of research.[48]

Replacing staff can be costly in terms of advertising, training and the time of both managers and recruitment staff. Cascio (2003) suggested that turnover costs can easily run to 1.5–2.5 times the salary of the person being replaced, depending on the job.[49] So, for example, if you have to replace a worker whose salary is $90,000, the costs of replacing that person could be $135,000, and up to $225,000 for high-performing staff.

There is one other reason why managers should consider keeping their workforce happy: social responsibility. Much of the focus on social responsibility

---

43 Ledford (1999), p. 27.
44 Liszka, J. (2005). 'Why Happiness is of Marginal Value in Ethical Decision-making'. *Journal of Value Inquiry*, 39(3–4), 325–44, p. 333.
45 Curkendall, S., Ruiz, K.M., Joish, V. and Mark, T.L. (2010). 'Productivity Losses among Treated Depressed Patients Relative to Healthy Controls'. *Journal of Occupational & Environmental Medicine*, 52(2), 125–30.
46 Fisher, V.E. and Hanna, J.V. (1931). *The Dissatisfied Worker*, New York: Macmillan.
47 Hom, P.W. and Griffith, R.W. (1995). *Employee Turnover*, Cincinnati, OH: South/Western.
48 Wright and Bonett (2007).
49 Cascio, W.F. (2003). *Managing Human Resources: Productivity, Quality of Life, Profits*, 6th edn, New York: McGraw-Hill.

at business schools is on the external environment, but the area where you as manager have the greatest impact on welfare is on your workers.

The need for a shift from the external to internal environment is becoming greater. Hosie and Sevastos (2009) state that approximately one in ten workers are estimated to be suffering from depression, anxiety, stress or burnout in Australia, the European Union, the USA and Canada.[50] The World Health Organization has warned that psychological depression is reaching epidemic proportions, and by 2020 will be the second-largest killer in the world, behind heart disease. Workplace pressures and strains are an important determinant of a person's mental health. If managers want to be truly social responsible, they should focus on management and their knowledge of human nature.

Managers can do much to increase the self-esteem, identity and sense of belonging among their staff. Improving competencies and reducing absenteeism and turnover do not just contribute to financial performance. When workers have high-quality interactions with their organization, supervisors and co-workers, they have enhanced well-being. When workers feel committed to their workplace, they experience greater job satisfaction and mental and physical well-being, perform better in the workplace and are less likely to leave their jobs.[51] In 2007, Wright and Bonett noted: 'It is becoming increasingly evident to many that promoting employee PWB [psychological well-being] and satisfaction is an intrinsic good for which all should work.'[52]

The emphasis on social responsibility has led to a need to understand the broader impact of a manager's actions on society, but the place where managers have the most impact is in the community they manage – their community of workers. With this in mind, a management approach that focuses on human nature suggests that if you want to make the world a better place, focus on being a better manager.

50 Hosie, P.J. and Sevastos, P. (2009). 'Does the "Happy-productive Worker" Thesis Apply to Managers?'. *International Journal of Workplace Health Management*, 2(2), 131–60.
51 Ladebo, O.J., Olaoye, O.J. and Adamu, C.O. (2008). 'Extension Personnel's Self-esteem and Workplace Relationships: Implications for Job Satisfaction and Affective Organizational Commitment Foci'. *Journal of Agricultural Education and Extension*, 14(3), 249–63.
52 Wright and Bonett (2007), p. 155.

Index

Page numbers in **bold** refer to figures and tables.